THE PLANTPOWER WAY

THE PLANTPOWER WAY

WHOLE FOOD PLANT-BASED RECIPES AND GUIDANCE FOR THE WHOLE FAMILY

RICH ROLL AND JULIE PIATT

AVERY

an imprint of Penguin Random House · New York

CONTENTS

ICON LEGEND

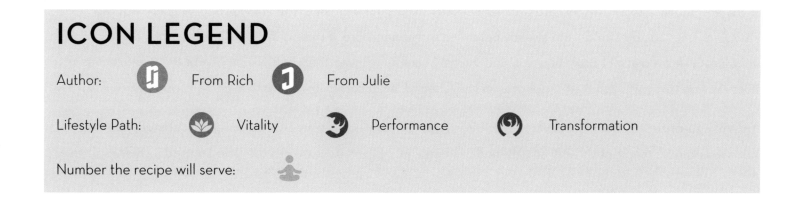

Author: 🜨 From Rich　　🜨 From Julie

Lifestyle Path: 🌱 Vitality　　🐦 Performance　　🕊 Transformation

Number the recipe will serve: 🧘

FOREWORD

By CNN Chief Medical Correspondent Sanjay Gupta, MD

It would be too easy to call this a book of recipes or a guide to go vegan. It is much more than that. It is an invitation to be a guest at the home of a truly marvelous family. As you know, one can learn quite a lot about people through the foods they consume, and you will feel like you are part of this family by the time you are done with *The Plantpower Way*. Julie, Rich, and their kids—Tyler, Trapper, Mathis, and Jaya—are all ridiculously fit, good-looking, and oozing bliss. They share a lot of themselves in this book and seamlessly weave together their stories, their philosophy, and their food—the final product feels wonderfully complete, authentic, and delicious. Quite simply, Julie Piatt and Rich Roll have authored the best book I have read on the topic, and I have read many. *The Plantpower Way* is remarkably thorough, teaches you about the very essence of the foods, provides a guide to buying those foods, and includes the perfect preparation and the astonishing benefits. There are big lessons and small, such as when to add herbs and spices for maximum return, and also a reminder to take time to *smell those herbs* every now and then.

The book quickly jumps onto your wavelength and is so intuitive that it provides answers before you even ask the question. To blend or to juice. How to get your kids on the diet and the age-old query about whether plants can provide adequate protein. In case your curiosity is piqued, Rich Roll says you can absolutely get the building blocks of protein you need through Plantpower, and decrease the risk of vascular disease at the same time. He will show you how.

By the way, I am living proof of his philosophy. It worked for me.

If you are perusing this book, you are probably already looking for a change. You are likely dissatisfied with the *standard American diet* (SAD) and already believe in something more. If that sounds familiar, this book could change your life. Give it a place of prominence in your home. Share it with your friends. It will be one of the greatest gifts you ever provide. They will definitely thank you for the Cherry Cacao Blend; it is almost too good to be true.

This may surprise you, but most doctors didn't learn nutrition in medical school. It seems almost absurd, given that our foods can be medicine. Nearly all I learned has been on my own. And around the time I turned forty it took on a new sense of urgency. With heart disease running in my family, I was not prepared to accept the same destiny as generations of men before me. Not only did I want to avoid that seemingly preordained fate, I wanted to turn it on its head. I wanted to get fitter, healthier, and even younger than I was the year before. I spent late nights reading and then traveling the world to meet the people who could teach me even more. Rich Roll was one of the first people on my list.

Rich Roll is one of America's most admired athletes. It is not because he is an ultraman, which makes most people tired just describing it. It is not because he has clocked top finishes at the world championships. It is not because he is one of the world's fittest men, and one of the humblest at the same time. It is not even because he accomplished all of this on a plant-based diet. It is because he is just like you, and me.

He was sedentary and overweight at age forty, and believed he could be better. At a time when shortcuts and "hacks" had become the new normal, Rich worked incredibly hard and *invested in the journey*. It paid off.

No, this is not your typical recipe book. It is a book about hope, and the universally shared belief that any one of us can be better.

The book is also a story about unwavering support, steadfast faith, and love. Julie Piatt has spent decades perfecting the content of this book. She also spent countless hours developing strategies to nourish the body and the soul of her ultraman when he returned from his high-intensity training rides. From energy bars to green drinks to the perfect vegan brunch, it is all in here. If you ever considered a plant-based diet while training, this book is essential.

A few years ago, I had the good fortune of eating in the Malibu home of Julie and Rich. You will see the pictures of this magical place sprinkled throughout the book. It was an outstanding meal, and I didn't miss meat or dairy one bit. Even more powerful, though, was the infectious enthusiasm and support of the hosts themselves. Through *The Plantpower Way*, you will get to experience all of it for yourself.

I take immense pride in helping introduce the world to Rich Roll and Julie Piatt through a television story. As a health journalist, I have never found it sufficient to simply report on better ways to manage disease. And it wasn't good enough to simply preach wellness. I believe in the *optimization* of the human body and the human spirit. You will not find better guides in that quest than the authors of *The Plantpower Way*.

My friends Rich and Julie are going to help a lot of people become better versions of themselves through this book— and create a lot of joy along the way.

LET'S GET PLANTPOWERED!

Now Is the Time to Embrace the Next Level of Nutrition to Live Your Best Life

If this book is anything, it's a family celebration of just how dramatically our lives have changed in the last decade.

Eight years ago, enslaved by a dehumanizing career track dominated by eighty-hour workweeks, Rich was hurtling into a disillusioned middle-aged malaise. He had a hopeless addiction to fast food and a myriad of unhealthy lifestyle habits that left him fifty pounds overweight and on an inevitable crash course with depression, obesity, heart disease, and, ultimately, an early grave.

Eventually, Rich's pain became so great that he found a way out. When his bloated body was defeated by a simple flight of stairs on the eve of his fortieth birthday, Rich was struck with a profound moment of clarity precipitated by labored breathing, a sweaty brow, and acute tightness in his chest—not only did he need to change, he finally wanted to change.

By contrast, Julie has always been the healthy example in our relationship. Raised in Alaska on game meat delivered by the hands of her adventuresome, bush pilot father and prepared by her proper Chilean mother, she is an expert in many things—a lifelong yogi, spiritual guide, artist, chef, musician, and mother. But the essence of her life can be defined by a singular pursuit: the unrelenting quest to continually expand the horizons of her mind, body, and spirit.

As Rich lay awake in bed that night after his staircase episode, he was reminded of how some years prior Julie had used the principles of Ayurveda—a system of alternative medicine derived from ancient Hindu culture that promotes balance through stress reduction and a predominantly plant-based diet—to completely heal and eradicate a golf ball–size cyst in her neck.

This miraculous event confounded the medical specialists consulted, all of whom emphatically professed that Julie's condition could never be resolved without surgery. The inexplicability of this phenomenon had always perplexed Rich's unfailingly logic-oriented, Stanford-trained brain. But that night Rich's thoughts turned instead to the sagacious words uttered by Hippocrates more than 2,300 years ago:

Let food be thy medicine and
medicine be thy food.

The answer was clear. This simple yet prophetic statement catalyzed a fantastic, revolutionary, and evolutionary family voyage we continue to explore, refine, and reimagine to this day. An odyssey in healthy, rejuvenating, whole, plant-based foods that recalibrated every aspect of Rich's life and birthed a foundational template for healthy, sustainable lifestyle practices that can be embraced and enjoyed by the entire family.

Fueled by Julie's original, beautiful, delicious, and incredibly nutritious food creations, which you'll find in this book, Rich quickly dropped the weight, resumed a fitness regimen for the first time in many years, and went on to achieve astounding feats of middle-aged athleticism he could have never previously fathomed. Two years later, Rich had transformed from a chubby couch potato to being named one of the "25 Fittest Men in the World" by *Men's Fitness* magazine after a top finish at the Ultraman World Championships, a 320-mile double-ironman distance triathlon widely considered one of the most grueling endurance challenges on the planet. A year later, Rich accomplished the unimaginable when he was the first person (along with friend Jason Lester) to complete the EPIC5: five Ironman-distance triathlons on five separate Hawaiian Islands in under seven days. That's 703 miles of swimming, biking, and running in less than a week!

Inspired by Rich's sea change, Julie continued to push the boundaries of conventional wisdom in the kitchen, creating a litany of fantastically appetizing, wholesome, easy-to-prepare, budget-conscious recipes to fuel her athlete husband and please four children's finicky palates.

It's been eight years since our amazing journey began. There have been unimaginable highs matched by countless low lows as we faced insurmountable obstacles while blazing a new lifestyle path for ourselves and our children premised not on fear and insecurity, but rather on faith, experience, and adventure. It's our bold experiment in living from the heart.

With a focus on service to others struggling with their own evolution/revolution, we made a conscious decision to share our journey openly with a terrifying level of transparency and vulnerability that often left us wondering if our version of courage just might be foolishness.

However, the outpouring of support has been nothing short of staggering. Lighting our path through the dark times were the thousands of deeply inspiring e-mails that flooded our inbox from all corners of the world—people from all walks of life sharing the intimate details of their own monumental health and lifestyle transformations catalyzed by adopting their personal versions of our "Plantpowered" way of life.

The scope of these shared life transformations is beyond extraordinary—dramatic weight loss; freedom from cholesterol and blood pressure medications; notable athletic accomplishments; and the reversal of chronic health conditions such as atherosclerosis, diabetes, fibromyalgia, migraines, asthma, arthritis, urticaria, autoimmune disorders, and intestinal illnesses such as Crohn's disease, irritable bowel syndrome, and ulcerative colitis.

Even more profound are the many tales of spiritual awakening. We all know that surrounding ourselves with positive-minded people can favorably impact how we perceive the world around us. Food is no different. It, too, is energy, carrying a certain vibration—a charge that can be positive or negative. Indeed, the nature of the frequency we ingest has an indelibly profound impact on every aspect of how we feel, interact, behave, comprehend, and appreciate the world around us.

Food is not just a reparative nourishment for our physical bodies; it is a vehicle for improving clarity of thought. It is a key to unlock the soul to ponder new horizons of personal possibility—and ultimately pave the road to discover, unlock, and unleash your best, most authentic self. *This is what this book is truly about.*

What this book isn't? A "*diet*" book. Because diets don't work. Intuitively we all know this to be true. When the honeymoon period ends—and it always does—we fall off the wagon. Of course we want to look and feel better, thus we continue to search for a sustainable wellness solution that will work within the constraints of our increasingly busy professional and family lives. So time and again, we naively buy into irresistible weight-loss marketing hype, only to find the solution temporary at best. Failing again, we despair. Ultimately, all too many of us give up on the truth that has been staring us in the face all along: *sustainable long-term wellness is always well within our grasp.*

Personally, we're fed up with all the hype, hyperbole, pseudoscience, and misinformation surrounding diet, health, weight loss, and disease. Tired of marketing campaigns that relentlessly dupe us into subscribing to unhealthy and unsustainable lifestyle patterns. Sick of being manipulated into buying products we don't need, most of which quite ironically only lead us toward—rather than away from—a life of enslavement to the pharmaceutical companies and a litany of avoidable chronic illnesses that unnecessarily plague modern society.

It's time to stop the insanity. There must be a better way. And we're here to tell you there is. A straightforward back-to-basics solution that will repair, restore, energize, and invigorate your body, mind, and soul beyond what you might think possible. And it all begins and ends with one simple word: ***plants.***

Eating plant-based is neither a fad nor a momentary fashion trend, but rather a deep, lasting, sustainable lifestyle that can and will transform your life and the life of your children. *This is our promise.*

The best part? It's just not that hard. In fact, it can be fun. That's been our experience. And it can be yours, too.

If this all seems like a utopian fantasy, trust in the process. Start slow and lean in at your own pace. Pay close attention to how new foods make you feel. And understand that your body will indeed begin to make the shift for you. As we often say, transformation is in the gut. Replacing the animal products and processed foods with nourishing, organic, locally grown fruits, vegetables, legumes, nuts, and seeds will begin to alter the ecology of your intestinal microbial population. Science proves a powerful nexus between the nature of your gut flora and the foods you crave. So don't be surprised if your previously uncontrollable lust for unhealthy foods begins to dissipate, miraculously replaced with a craving for the foods that invigorate rather than enervate.

Food shouldn't just be fun to eat; it should also be fun to prepare and share. This book is about restoring this tradition. It's about elevating the enjoyment, conversation, laughter, and cooperation that accompanies one of the great pleasures in life: *the family meal*—precious, fleeting moments every parent cherishes as essential to promoting optimal health for ourselves and our children.

Throughout this book we present more than 120 original recipes we ourselves eat on a continual rotation. In addition, each recipe is labeled with an icon in accordance with one of three paths we've designed to customize your meal planning based on your interests and desired results: **Vitality** (food for balance and harmony), **Performance** (food for physical excellence), or **Transformation** (food for rebirth). Refer to pages 298–308 if you are interested in a more focused plan; otherwise, enjoy the recipes in this book however you'd like.

Throughout the book are additional materials on the specifics of nutrition, strategies for improving your children's food habits, and insights into the often highly charged emotional landscape that surrounds food choice, creativity as a spiritual life force, ecological conditions related to our food supply, and our collective, shared responsibility as sensible stewards for the sustainable health of our children, brothers, sisters, fellow animals, and the planet as a whole.

Finally, our hope is that you use this book as a guide—a foundational platform to jump off and create your own unique way of living. Take what serves you and discard the rest, as every life is vastly unique and individualized. Our journey will not look exactly like yours. But our sincere hope is that we can help inspire you along your own path.

We leave you with this: we are all capable of so much more than we allow ourselves to be. The path to unlocking our inner potential starts with what we put in our mouths. So let's hit reset. Let's begin anew the process of stepping into that person we always wanted, and deserve, to be.

We did it. And you can, too. So let's not waste any more time and get to living.

Peace + Plants,

Rich, Julie, Tyler, Trapper, Mathis & Jaya

⑴ BEGINNING THE JOURNEY

The first step in embracing a Plantpowered lifestyle is getting back to basics. This means making space in your life for a rotating seasonal variety of whole, plant-based foods in their natural state, just the way Mother Nature intended.

Don't freak out. Eating plant-based isn't a life sentence of salad leaf dinners. And we're not proposing that "raw" necessarily means healthier for every person, every day, and every meal. But ask yourself this: *When was the last time you served a veggie on your table without first boiling the life out of it or baking it into oblivion?* Have you taken the time to really get acquainted with the foods that are being grown in your area? Do you know which produce is in season and what new local food possibilities exist for you?

We certainly didn't have answers to these questions when we started our journey. But we've learned a few things. Let's take a closer look:

First: *stop overcooking your food!* In the most general terms, this significantly diminishes overall nutritional value. Zapping away the good stuff, prolonged heat can degrade micronutrient density and can damage some vitamins and minerals. The result? Limp, bland, and tasteless plants unnecessarily deficient in the nourishing *life force* we want to welcome.

Second: *stop buying plants out of season!* Just because you can buy peaches 365 days a year doesn't mean it's the right thing for your body or the planet. The truth is that a seasonal rotation of plant variety in your diet is a cornerstone of maximum, long-term wellness and optimal functionality.

Eating the same vegetables and fruits year-round both in and out of season can lead to food allergies and sensitivities that negatively impact health. Moreover, eating produce out of season has a gigantic carbon footprint. Growing a pineapple in Hawaii that will be eaten during a snowstorm in New Jersey is vastly wasteful and ecologically irresponsible. Furthermore, that pineapple is not doing you much good anyway, because it was likely picked weeks earlier and thus is far from "fresh," organic or otherwise. Finally, eating "summer plants" in the dead of winter is counter-intuitive. It's what a philosophy of eastern Indian medicine called Ayurveda would deem *dosha aggravating*—out of balance with the natural rhythms of the body.

Third: *no one food is a panacea!* Our culture is hell-bent on extremes. We read that kale is

healthy, so what do we do? We all run over to the kale side of the boat and start gorging. Then we're surprised when the boat tips over and we are all drowning in vitamin K. But wasn't kale supposed to be good? Yes, but not if you are choking on it at the expense of nutritional variety.

It's important to remember that even if you live in a city and work in a skyscraper, you are not exempt from nature and the rhythms of our global ecosystem. As responsible stewards of our bodies and the planet, it's crucial that our choices and actions are harmoniously aligned with this grand play. Mother Nature created thousands of edible plant varieties that grow at different times of the year. It's time to start getting better at following this natural cycle of food.

In the following sections, we offer only an introduction to some of the amazing whole foods that are available for our nourishment.

FRUITS + VEGETABLES

Mother Nature provides an astounding variety of fruits and vegetables for our health and well-being. The key to healthy plant-based nutrition is to enjoy a broad diversity of these wonderful plants in all their vibrant colors. Go ahead! Experiment and explore foods you've never tasted before. Celebrate fruits and veggies in their pure, natural, and untouched state as part of your plant-based plates. It's as easy as a peach or as crispy as a carrot. Organic, locally harvested, and homegrown varieties make for the highest nutritional value and are always the best choices for living in harmony with nature. Create your own personal rainbow of "amazing" that will deliver you into a life of vibrant health.

LIVING HERBS

Living herbs are aromatic healers that uplift your meals and everyone around them. Use herbs generously at every meal. We prefer adding them at the end of the cooking process so that they remain crisp, fresh, and alive. Herbs make the best kind of natural healing teas, lift the vibrancy up a notch in your blend, and beautify your plate. Our advice? Take some time to smell them and absorb their gifts of healing aromas.

GRAINS + LEGUMES

There are so many beautiful grains and legumes flourishing on this planet, foods naturally designed to nourish our bodies. But today's wheat is not your grandmother's wheat. Modern wheat is overwhelmingly hybridized, nutritionally deficient, and brimming with gluten—sticky, glue-like protein that is causing health imbalances for many. We encourage you to experiment with healthier, gluten-free alternative grains like millet, amaranth, teff, buckwheat, sorghum, rice, and quinoa (technically a seed and high in protein). Stuck on wheat? Then opt for the "heirloom" variety. These so-called heritage or ancient grain varietals are non-hybridized, higher in nutritional value than traditional wheat, and arguably safer for the gluten-sensitive. In addition to being high in protein and low in fat, legumes such as dried beans and lentils are great base ingredients for warming chili, our one-bowl macro meals, and veggie burgers. To significantly amplify the nutritional value of your beans and grains, try sprouting them at home (see page 10).

NUTS + SEEDS

Sacred gifts from trees and plants, nuts and seeds brim with crucial nutrients and provide a delicious spectrum of tastes and luscious textures to enliven your Plantpowered lifestyle. Raw almonds, walnuts, cashews, and Brazil nuts are packed with healthy nutrients, perk up many a dish, and make for a sumptuous snack on the go. However, if you have nut allergies or heart disease, or if weight loss is a priority, then skip the nuts (which have higher fat content) and opt instead for seeds such as pumpkin or sesame. Then take your routine to the next level with superfood seeds like chia, hemp, and ground flax to exhilarate your salads and turbocharge your smoothies. Soak your nuts and seeds first to ease assimilation. A source of high-density nutrition and vibrant energy, nuts and seeds will help you create beautiful foods with an exotic, luxurious flair. From delectable raw pie crusts to creamy sauces and frothy milks, seeds and nuts are the perfect ingredients to vitalize your plant-based journey.

❶ SPROUTING

Sprouting bumps nuts, grains, beans, and seeds into the realm of living vibrant foods by enhancing nutritional density and the bioavailability of the plant's vitamins, minerals, proteins, fiber, enzymes, essential fatty acids, and phytochemicals to create a higher level of healthy nourishment.

As we evolve to incorporate more living foods into our diet, I find that sprouting makes for a fresher, more alive taste, adding extra flair to my recipes. Highly alkalizing and anti-inflammatory, sprouted foods have been linked to everything from disease prevention to improved digestion.

Therefore, I always prefer sprouted over regular tofu and sprouted, gluten-free flour varieties in my baked goods. Sprouted grains are lower in starch and the gluten that causes digestion issues for so many. Rich in iron, mung bean sprouts combat anemia and are LDL-cholesterol reducing. Plus, sprouted beans cause less gas, easing digestion. High in antioxidants called sulphoraphanes, broccoli sprouts are even considered cancer-preventive and help regulate blood sugar.

At first, I felt overwhelmed by the idea of sprouting anything. It just seemed like such a huge ordeal, so I would buy sprouted beans at the farmers' market and grocery stores whenever I could. But finally I got the courage to give sprouting a try at home. After some trial and error, I discovered an efficient method easy for any kitchen novice. Now sprouting is an integral part of my weekly cooking preparation.

Here's How I Do It

First, you will need three colanders, each lined with a flour sack or cotton dishcloth along the bottom, large enough to fold over the top. These are your "sprouting stations." Add your preferred grain, seed, bean, or nut to each station.

I like to leave my stations out on our kitchen counter so I can rinse them frequently throughout the day whenever I happen to pass by. It takes only a moment to rinse them thoroughly and let the water drain out.

After each rinsing, I cover the fledgling sprouts by folding the excess ends of the liner cloth over the top. Using this process, sprouting takes two to three days, depending on the size of the grain, seed, nut, or legume.

When the seeds are finally sprouted, transfer them to mason jars, seal, label, and refrigerate. Kept cold, they will remain fresh for up to a week.

Remember: Sprouting makes your quantities expand. Use 1 cup of beans and you'll end up with double the volume.

A Small Word of Caution

Prior to eating, always smell your sprouts; throw them out if you detect anything that smells like mold. The scent should be clear and clean like a fresh veggie. Also, be a little careful with raw legume sprouts—they may have some toxicity (this doesn't apply to the broccoli or daikon sprouts that we enjoy in salads and sandwiches, which are fine to eat raw). For this reason, just to be safe, I always cook my sprouted beans, which I love using in recipes such as our Black Bean Soup (page 158), Veggie Burgers (page 199), Sprouted Mung Kicheri (page 162), and macro One Bowls (page 197).

SUPERFOODS FOR THE WIN

10 High-Performance Foods for Next-Level Wellness & Athletic Excellence

Throughout my twenties and thirties, I abused my body with a revolving door of junk food, drugs, alcohol, and pretty much anything I could find to numb my discontentment. Overhauling my diet played a crucial role in my midlife transformation. In the most general sense, fruits and vegetables repaired my body wholesale, but there's more to the story.

I am not a professional athlete. But over several years, I managed to balance a life of twenty- to thirty-hour training weeks and crazy endurance events with my (now former) career as an entertainment lawyer, my busy family life, and of course writing books like this one.

And yet despite the significant physical, professional, mental, and emotional demands of my everyday life, I can't recall the last time I got sick or missed a workout, family obligation, or professional deadline because I was too tired. And despite my advancing age, I continue to improve as an athlete—getting leaner, stronger, and faster with each successive year. How is this possible?

Superfoods.

Admittedly, the term is subject to cavalier overuse. And the purported health benefits are frequently overblown. I get it. But through personal experimentation, I am convinced that my steady intake of the plants listed on the following pages (some uncommon, others more mainstream) has played a significant role in helping me break the glass ceiling on my physical potential.

To be clear, superfoods should never be considered miraculous cure-alls. Instead, think of them as the cherry atop the sundae—the final 1 percent in your personal nutritional evolution + revolution. In other words, if your diet is lousy—low in nutrient density; high in salt, sugar, fat, and artificial additives; and over processed—then superfoods are not the solution to what ails you. So before you fork over your hard-earned cash on the below items—some of which are admittedly expensive—use this book (as well as the appendix materials of *Finding Ultra*) to master the basics of healthy eating before you dabble in discovering the impact of superfoods.

There already? Great! Now let's play. . . .

1. Chia Seeds

If you've read the best-selling book *Born to Run*, then you know these tiny seeds are an ancient Aztec staple known as the "ultimate runner's food" for their ability to increase oxygen uptake, impede dehydration, and provide sustained energy over long periods of time.

Gelatinous when soaked in water, chia seeds are also non-GMO, gluten-free, anti-inflammatory, and high in antioxidants, and have been shown to reduce blood pressure and LDL cholesterol. In addition, chia seeds are a significant source of bioavailable dietary protein (14 percent by weight with a good balance of amino acids) and fiber (11 grams per ounce). Moreover, they are high in phytonutrients, electrolytes, and trace minerals, aiding bone health. In fact, just 1 ounce (about 2 tablespoons) contains 18 percent of your RDA of calcium and 30 percent of your RDA of magnesium.

One of the big critiques of a plant-based diet is that it is deficient in healthy omega-3 EFAs (essential fatty acids). Nonsense. Plenty of plant-based foods are packed with this important nutrient, and chia seeds are one of them. In fact, by weight chia seeds contain more omega-3s than salmon.

Finally, this tiny seed is highly utilitarian. Add a tablespoon to your morning blend; sprinkle them on your breakfast cereal; create puddings; and add them to your salads or rice and vegetable dishes for an extra superfood kick.

2. Hemp Seeds

First let's dispel the elephant in the room. This seed, and other hemp-related nutritional products like hemp oil and hemp protein, does not contain THC (tetrahydrocannabinol) and will not cause you to fail a drug test. So put your mind at ease.

While they will not alter your consciousness, these little white seeds are packed with health benefits. Much like chia, they are high in omega-3 EFAs, dietary fiber, and important minerals including iron and calcium.

In addition, hemp seeds are also considered a fantastic source of bioavailable, high-quality protein. With 33 percent protein by weight, 3 tablespoons contain 11 grams of protein—higher than any other nutritious seed.

Hemp seed consumption can prevent arterial plaque buildup and reduce blood pressure, cholesterol, and fatigue while increasing sustained energy, immune system functionality, and circulation. The significant anti-inflammatory and antioxidant properties of these tiny seeds have also been shown to expedite physiological recovery and repair from disease, injury, and exercise-induced stress.

Pick up a bag of shelled hemp seeds at your local health market or online, and don't miss an opportunity to add a tablespoon or two to your morning smoothies, salads, cereals, and vegetable dishes.

3. SPIRULINA

One of the most nutritious concentrated food sources on the planet, spirulina is a freshwater blue-green algae (actually, it's a cyanobacteria) noted for having the highest percentage of protein by weight of any food on Earth (50 to 70 percent by weight, with red meat clocking in at around 27 percent). Moreover, the protein is highly digestible, bioavailable, and considered "complete" because it contains all the essential amino acids.

Spirulina is rich in a wide variety of vitamins, phytonutrients, and antioxidants, and studies have established a strong correlation between spirulina intake and enhanced endurance, as well as expedited recovery induced by exercise stress.

Spirulina's additional purported health benefits are expansive. It promotes a systemic reduction in inflammation, enhances eye health, reduces total cholesterol, boosts HDL, improves liver function, reduces risk of stroke, and has been demonstrated effective in treating allergies, as well as asthma.

Available in both powder and liquid form, spirulina is a daily addition to my morning green smoothie.

4. *Cordyceps* (*Sinensis*) Extracts

Well-known for centuries in Chinese herbal medicine, *Cordyceps sinensis* is a parasitic dried fungus that grows on caterpillar larvae native to high-altitude regions of China, Nepal, and Tibet. Gross, right? But awesome when it comes to health and athletic performance. Pharmacologically antioxidative, anti-inflammatory, and anti-lipid (cholesterol lowering), studies indicate that it enhances immune system functionality as well as improves stamina in endurance athletes via increasing aerobic capacity and oxygen utilization, as well as stabilizing blood sugar metabolism. Chinese Olympic track & field athletes have been swearing by it for decades, and I can attest to its effectiveness. Another plus? Increased sex drive and functionality. The benefits of *Cordyceps* are enhanced when combined with the adaptogen rhodiola.

I mix *Cordyceps* in powder form in my preworkout smoothies and juices and often in my postworkout blends as well.

5. Turmeric

If you like curry, you're already familiar with this yellow plant native to South India and Indonesia. What you might not know is that turmeric—due in large part to curcumin, turmeric's primary active ingredient—is one of the most powerful antioxidants and anti-inflammatories on the planet.

The majority of foods we eat, including ones in low-fat diets, promote arterial inflammation, which is a leading (and often underrated) cause of heart disease. In the fitness context, exercise-induced physiological stress causes inflammation, which impedes muscle repair. In a general sense, the more quickly the inflammation subsides, the more quickly one recovers from training. Foods like turmeric reduce inflammation, thus expediting recovery (and circulatory health). Extrapolated over time, an athlete on a nutritional regimen high in antioxidants and anti-inflammatory foods such as turmeric (buttressed by a predominantly alkaline-forming diet) will in turn be able to train harder, more effectively, and more efficiently in a given time period while simultaneously taking out an insurance policy against the primary culprits that foil even the most conscientious athletes—undue fatigue, overtraining, and illness.

Furthermore, it's worth noting that there is some evidence to suggest that people who eat diets rich in turmeric have lower rates of breast, prostate, lung, colon, and skin cancers.

Curcumin can be taken in capsule form, but it is not the most bioavailable substance in extract form. Personally, I prefer to drink turmeric in a tea—½ teaspoonful dissolved in hot water does the trick.

6. Green Coffee Beans

Similar to green tea and grape seed extract, organic raw (green) coffee beans have powerful anti-inflammatory and antioxidant properties effective in combating free radical damage. There are also weight-management benefits due to two active compounds: caffeine and chlorogenic acid. The caffeine releases fatty acids into the bloodstream from stored body fat. The chlorogenic acid, which is destroyed in typical coffee beans by the roasting process, increases the efficiency of metabolizing these fats while inhibiting sugar (glucose) absorption by the bloodstream.

Simply grind the green beans and prepare in a French press like normal coffee. Alternatively, place the ground beans in water in the sun to brew iced coffee. However, don't expect it to taste like coffee—it doesn't. Nor will it give you the same kind of boost; its caffeine content is significantly lower than that of roasted beans. Try adding erythritol to sweeten the slightly bitter and somewhat flavorless drink.

7. Suma Root & the 4 Ginseng Blend

Adaptogens are metabolic regulators that increase the body's ability to—for lack of a better phrase—adapt to environmental stressors, both physical and emotional. Suma is a ginseng-like adaptogen extracted from a root native to Brazil that is linked to improved immune system functionality and hormonal regulation. Combine with (American) ginseng, ashwagandha (Indian ginseng), and *Eleutherococcus* (Siberian ginseng) to create a potent combination that promotes longevity and stress management—normalizing and balancing emotional and physical energy levels. Take in capsules (easily sourced online) or brew into a tea.

8. Camu Camu

A sour lemon-size orange-purple fruit indigenous to Amazonian lowlands, camu camu contains an impressive array of phytochemicals, bioflavonoids, amino acids, vitamins, and minerals like beta-carotene and potassium. Most important, camu camu boasts the highest natural vitamin C density of any food on the planet—anywhere from twenty to fifty times the level of vitamin C in a typical orange, and scores extremely high on the ORAC (oxygen radical absorbance capacity) scale, a method of quantifying the antioxidant capacities of biological samples. Camu camu also reduces levels of the stress hormone cortisol and facilitates the uptake of serotonin. In other words, it will make you happy.

Available in supplement form, I like Navitas Naturals Organic Camu Powder. Add a teaspoon to a cup of juice or a smoothie (the taste is tart, a bit like orange juice itself).

9. MORINGA OLEFIERA

Dubbed the "miracle tree" and the "world's most nutritious plant species ever studied," this amazing tree is native to regions of Africa and Asia but can grow almost anywhere due to its incredible ability to extract nutrients from the soil and air. Its leaves are an all-around green superfood; with more than ninety nutrients, moringa is like a utility baseball player who can excel in every position. High in a wide array of vitamins and minerals, it's antioxidant rich (forty-six antioxidants), anti-diabetes (reduces blood glucose), and promotes heart health (lipid lowering), among other benefits.

Available in capsule and powder form, brew it into a tea or add it to juice or your morning smoothie.

10. PU-ERH TEA

This tea can be perhaps the most expensive in the world, with some cakes priced at $350k (for a 250-gram cake), its leaves derived from trees that are hundreds of years old. A post-fermented tea product produced in the Yunnan province of China and carefully aged, the harvesting, creation, and ceremony of Pu-erh is an art steeped in preserved tradition dating back millennia.

But what makes Pu-erh truly unique is the process by which the leaves are fermented by microbes after drying and then aged. It is believed that the microbial activity in the tea provides probiotic health benefits unique to Pu-erh, such as reducing arterial plaque and LDL cholesterol levels as well as aiding weight loss by reducing blood sugar levels and improving the body's ability to metabolize fat. Pu-erh teas I've tried provide a long-lasting, even-keeled energy.

Very affordable versions of Pu-erh are widely available—I recommend checking out Living Tea (livingtea.net). To learn more, I suggest you consult your local teahouse. There is nothing like a traditional Pu-erh tea ceremony administered by a tea master. It's an extraordinary experience.

To Test or Not to Test?

All well and good, I hear you saying. But where's the proof? Therein lies the rub. To be sure, studies of varying legitimacy exist to substantiate the above. But large-scale, peer-reviewed research requires substantial funding. This funding is often provided by for-profit corporations that have little interest in validating natural products that cannot be protected via patents.

That said, I'm not asking you to take my word for it. Do your own research. Experiment. Start conservatively, document your findings, and tweak your way to success.

3 FERMENTED FOODS
Your "Gut" Instinct

The microbial environment living inside you is made up of trillions of bacteria—three to four pounds, in fact! The quality of your gut microbiome has a huge influence on food cravings. Think of it as the macrocosm within the microcosm or the universe within. As you start to shift into eating more plant-based whole foods, this microbial population will transform and, along with it, so will your cravings. No joke. Because get this. It's not a head trip—it's all in your gut.

Probiotics are naturally occurring live microorganisms that line our gut. They assist us with healthy digestion and absorption of nutrients. Fermented foods like kombucha, sauerkraut, miso, tempeh, and kimchi promote a healthy gut ecology by providing probiotic digestive enzymes, increased nutrients, and enhanced immunity.

MASTER PLANTPOWER SHOPPING LIST

What's the first priority on the master list? Tons of plants! This can be in the form of many varieties of fruits and veggies. Make sure you've got all the colors of the rainbow covered and, whenever possible, shop locally, organically, and responsibly.

Learn how to read labels. Educate yourself about how and where your produce is grown. Research sources of heirloom grains and vegetables that are free from genetic modification. Veer away from processed wheat products and instead lean into gluten-free alternatives. Support your local farmers' markets. Shop in-season to cut down on your planetary footprint and reduce food sensitivities and allergies. Better yet, grow your own food!

Maybe the one most powerful thing you can do is give up processed refined sugars. Make no mistake—high-fructose corn syrup is toxic and it's hiding in most packaged foods. Taking this measure will help regulate blood sugar and insulin. Insulin is the hormone of longevity, so it's crucial to do what we can to optimize its functionality. Simply put, refined sugars have no place in your health equation.

Just as we write this list, our bodies are rejoicing in all the succulent, juicy, divine foods that are here to assist us in experiencing true health. Our mouths water as we envision all the vibrant health radiating from these foods!

In the pages that follow, we provide a list of the vast array of healing foods in the plant kingdom (it's by no means exhaustive!) as well as our favorite, everyday pantry staples:

Plantpower Up with Greens

Getting greens into your body daily is going to shift your internal microbial makeup faster than anything else we know of. As we always say, the best first step no matter where you are in your food journey is to get your greens on! The easiest way to do this is with a blend, but don't stop there—make sure at least several of these healers from the list below make it onto your plate at every meal!

Get Your Greens On!

Greens are typically high in vitamins K, A, and C. They are loaded with antioxidants, are anti-inflammatory, help support healthy bones, and improve brain function.

- Kale—all varieties: curly, dinosaur, purple.
- Swiss chard and chard—the chards are great sautéed and mixed with quinoa.
- Collard greens—use these large leaves to wrap untuna, hummus, or pesto.
- All lettuce varieties—the foundation of every great salad!
- Sprouts—all varieties. Note that broccoli sprouts lead in high nutrient content.
- Brussels sprouts—an acquired taste. Steam and splash with apple cider vinegar and sea salt … yum.
- Turnip and beet greens—can be sautéed just like chard.
- Arugula—loaded with vitamin K. Rich loves his with sea salt and balsamic drizzle.
- Dandelion greens—also of the spicy variety, use sparingly … or daringly.
- Mustard greens—these are uber spicy! You can use apple cider vinegar and sea salt to take the edge off.
- Spinach—add it to blends and salads for a great dose of vitamin A.

More Plantpower Veggies

These include both raw and cooked options.

- Cauliflower—chop this and season it with lively Mexican flavors to use in tacos and enchiladas, or steam and pour warm cashew cheese over the top.
- Carrots, red and golden beets, fennel, celery root—eat these raw or cooked, shredded or chopped in salads, or on their own.

- Red, yellow, orange, and green bell peppers—extremely high in vitamin C.
- Jalapeños and hot peppers—for a little kick, use the real thing instead of a bottled hot sauce.
- Cucumbers and celery—add a crunchy taste to any spread or salad.
- Green beans, asparagus, and artichokes—give them a healthy French note and serve with a nice Dijon sauce.

Healing Herbs & Roots

Many of us had mothers or grandmothers who used herbs and roots as healing remedies, but we may have lost that connection to nature. It's important to remember that these plants were designed to assist our bodies in vibrant health. Here is a list of some of these powerful healers:

- Dill—supports healthy digestion and can assist with insomnia. Julie loves her dill in potato salad. For a twist on our Untuna Wraps (page 229), try adding fresh dill.
- Mint—can fight against colon cancer and assists with asthma. It smells divine and makes a great tea and mint cacao pie.
- Cilantro—helps in detoxifying heavy metals from the body, so it's a must ingredient in our juices and blends. In many Mexican-inspired dishes it adds the "fresh" flavor. Also referred to as "coriander," many Indian-inspired dishes are graced with its presence.
- Oregano—a powerful healing herb that is anti-inflammatory and balancing, it has been used for centuries to heal many ailments. If you suffer from allergies, oregano oil may be your savior.
- Parsley—assists blood circulation and helps eliminate toxins. It also helps with bladder and kidney ailments. Julie loves it with watermelon, lemon, and apple cider vinegar to clear out those channels.
- Basil—an antiaging, anti-inflammatory addition to many a dish.
- Tulsi—used in Ayurveda for healing many imbalances, including reducing blood glucose levels.
- Fresh turmeric root—this is a natural anti-inflammatory antibiotic we use almost every day in our blends and juices.
- Fresh ginger—can lower blood pressure and cholesterol, reduce nausea, and aid digestion. It can also kick that cold. Juice ginger shots with a juice back at the onset of sniffles.

Special Notes About Garlic and Onions

- Garlic—we use this sparingly and more as medicine. If you have a cold or you are detoxifying your body, we suggest using generous amounts in a juice, blended drink, or soup. Otherwise, we use only very small amounts in the cheeses and sauces—not more than one clove. Or better yet, we often leave it out. Garlic is very stimulating and heating to the body. It's great if used in moderation or when you are sick or in need of detoxifying your system. Overuse can cause imbalances in your health.

• Onions—we also use onions very sparingly. Part of this is because we cook for children often. If we use them, our kids won't eat the meal! Also, we don't like the residue onions leave on the breath. We also learned that you should never eat a leftover onion because as soon as it's sliced, it begins to absorb airborne toxins. During the Black Plague of the Middle Ages, cut onions were placed in victims' rooms and the onions would actually turn black!

Plantpowered Fruits

• Avocado (Hass and Bacon)—this is one of the most nutritious fruits in the plant kingdom. Add these to salads or use them in blends or desserts for a creamy texture.

• Tomato—heirloom, cherry, Roma, and vine. A perfect addition to countless recipes.

• Tomatillo—green tomatoes that have a skin on them. We use these for our fresh green salsa. They aren't spicy so are a great option for children.

Citrus

• Lemon—we cook with lemons almost every meal. Despite tasting acidic, lemons actually have an alkalizing effect on the body, so they are super healers. Most meals can benefit from a squeeze at the final moment before serving. Use lemon in salad dressings and daily blends.

• Lime—contains electrolytes. Great for key lime pie or any Mexican-inspired dish, like salsas or black beans.

• Orange—great source of fiber. Antiaging and immunity building, oranges are high in vitamin C, potassium, and pectin.

• Grapefruit—a great source of vitamins C and A.

• Dates—from the palm tree, these come in many varieties and are our absolute favorite sweetener. This special fruit has been a great ally in creating great-tasting desserts.

• Grapes—freeze these and let the kids eat them as dessert!

• Figs—best picked from the tree. Eat both the skin and insides for a delicious, unique taste. We also like to lightly grill them and drizzle with Manuka honey or alternatively maple syrup. Top that off with hemp seeds and chopped mint.

• Apples—the kids make their own fresh juice from organic apples. Eaten raw, apples are great plaque removers. They also make great additions to any green and veggie blends.

• Pears—great sources of fiber. Try ripe juicy pears with a side of raw dates and walnuts. Squeeze a little lemon juice over the top to bring out the flavor.

Sweet Berries

This category is packed with healing properties. Get in the habit of eating a handful in the raw as often as you can or add frozen berries daily to your Plantpowered blends.

• Blueberries—among the highest-ranking antioxidants, blueberries are antiaging and improve cognitive function.

• Raspberries—neutralize free radicals and offer a delicate perfumed taste like no other.

• Strawberries—these are best eaten soon after they are picked to ensure their healing potency.

Choosing berries over desserts
with processed sugar will be a certain
game changer in your health.

• Blackberries—also ranking very high in antioxidants, blackberries can help prevent Alzheimer's and Parkinson's, are antiaging, and promote heart health by relaxing the arteries.

• Mulberries—used in Chinese medicine for thousands of years, these precious gifts can help with gray hair and insomnia.

• Goji berries—lower cholesterol and improve skin health. Some say eating these berries improves sexual functionality.

• Cherries—can improve sleep and help relieve the pain of arthritis and gout. They are also high on the antiaging spectrum.

Fungi

• Mushrooms—a healing staple of Chinese medicine for centuries. We love all varieties and source ours at the local farmers' market as a savory treat. Bold in taste, mushrooms are richly satisfying in gravies and risotto. Sauté them and serve over fresh crisp greens for a salad variation. With a little experimentation they will satisfy any "meat" comfort-food craving.

Tropical

• Coconut—considered the sacred fruit of the earth, coconut provides milk and meat loaded with nutrients deeply healing to the body. Its "water" is loaded with electrolytes and we use the "meat" for pies, cookies, blends, and many other recipes.

• Banana—great sources of potassium for the pesky muscle cramp, we use these in daily blends, puddings, and pie fillings. Sauté them in some coconut oil and drizzle maple syrup over the top for an exotic dessert.

• Pineapple—this fruit is loaded with vitamin C and can speed the healing of bruises. They are a great way to sweeten desserts naturally while fortifying your body with antioxidants.

• Mango—definitely a family favorite, one of the most unique tastes in the plant kingdom—a perfumed sweetness of the gods.

• Papaya—a digestion aid. These are best in raw form.

• Star fruit—these jewels are amazing works of art. Slicing them crosswise reveals little stars perfect for an edible garnish on desserts.

• Kiwi—loaded with vitamin C. Remove the skins and juice them for a great kids' juice. Juicing them removes the coarse texture of the seeds that can feel scratchy on the throat.

• Passion fruit—we recently learned about the hormone-balancing properties of the leaves from our friend and master gardener June Louks. If you have a fence and are in the right climate, you can easily grow a large patch of this amazing vine. The flowers are otherworldly and some varieties have a sweet nectar inside that you can sip like a hummingbird.

• Zapota—June's favorite dessert. She simply freezes them to eat right out of the skin! She also sweetens pies with this amazing fruit. If you live in a zone similar in climate to California, you may find a tree nearby, or plant your own.

• Cherimoya—this sweet, exotic, filling fruit is used in a Mexican recipe for a cool drink. Also best right out of the skin. We also use this as a preferred substitute for a little something sweet.

Sweet flavors nourish the
soul and replenish the spirit.

Beans

• Black beans—probably our favorite bean. We like to use them in our veggie burgers, Mexican-inspired dishes, chili, and soups.

• Adzuki beans—great to use in veggie burgers. They're smaller and take less time to cook from the dried form. We mash them between our fingers to get a smoother texture to mix with quinoa or rice.

• Mung beans—the healing bean of Ayurveda. We love sprouted mung beans in salads or soups and a healing stew called Sprouted Mung Kicheri (page 162). Our version is a great recipe to eat while you are cleansing or giving your body a rest from digesting heavy foods.

• Lentils—green, black, French—all varieties are great options.

• Asafoetida powder—also known as "hing," this Indian spice is derived from fennel and reminiscent of leeks. It's a digestive aid that reduces the gas in beans.

Rice

Many varieties serve as a foundation for many recipes: black, Arborio, short-grain brown, basmati, jasmine. When possible, opt for organic and heirloom varieties as there are recent reports of arsenic in conventionally harvested rice.

Pasta

A company called Explore makes some wonderful and nutritious non-wheat-based pastas, including mung bean fettuccine, black bean and adzuki spaghetti, and brown rice pad thai. They're packed with protein and are gluten-free. You'll love them (explore-asian.com).

Tofu

• Sprouted tofu—if we are eating tofu, it will always be sprouted and organic. We enjoy it occasionally, but due to conflicting health reports, we refrain from using it as an everyday high-protein meat replacement. Instead, look to whole plants and the list above. Don't worry about protein! There is more than enough protein in plants to meet your daily requirement (see But Where Do You Get Your Protein?, page 187).

• Silken tofu—this can make a smooth pudding or pie filling. But I prefer to get that texture using avocado. Once in a while, it can be a good substitute. But again, no need to overdo it here.

Coconut Cream (Canned)

We keep a few of these in the fridge chilled and ready to accent a plant-based ice cream dessert or as pie filling. It is so light and airy, you will feel energized after eating your dessert!

Frozen Organic Fruit—All Varieties

We always keep a few bags on hand for blends, ice cream, or just as a snack. Of course you can freeze your own excess fruit from your trees or farmers' market trips.

Secret Spices

The main spices we use comprise a short list. Julie can basically get around recipes pretty well with just these few.
- Sea salt—we like "Celtic" by Selina Naturally. There are other good varieties, but this is the one Julie won't cook without.
- Cinnamon—always great on oatmeal, yams, and in black bean chili and soups.
- Cumin (or chili powder, depending on spice preference)—also great for bean dishes and soups.
- Vanilla bean—this makes all the difference in that pie you are preparing and it will put your almond milk in a whole new category of amazing.

Garnishes

- Edible flowers—you can find these at your local healthy market or farmers' market, or in your own garden.
- Lavender, roses, and sage from the garden—these bring a deeper healing vibration into several of our recipes.

Milks

- Nut milks—made from almonds, cashews, walnuts, Brazil nuts, coconuts, sesame seeds, hemp seeds, and sunflower seeds. Buy it or make your own. You can find these recipes in our MILK + CHEESE section (page 66).

Oils

We prefer to cook with coconut oil as it maintains its integrity at high temperatures. Olive, hemp, grape seed, and macadamia nut oils are great in salads and provide much-needed essential fatty acids. *Note: use sparingly.* If you have heart health issues or are overweight, *cut out completely.*

Seasonings & Additives

• Nutritional yeast—used in our nut cheeses, to sprinkle over salads, and in blends. We use this often as it is a vital source of vitamin B_{12}.

• B_{12}—a crucial vitamin not readily found in the plant kingdom, it's the one supplement we recommend daily. Try our B_{12} spray, available at richroll.com.

• Miso paste—chickpea, brown rice, or soy. You'll find this in the cold section of your local market. We use miso in our nut cheese, sauces, dressings, and soups.

• Vegenaise or Just Mayo—these are both great non-dairy, egg-free mayonnaise alternatives that work great for our potato recipes and sandwiches. This definitely helps make the journey easier—but don't overuse the privilege.

• Gluten-free tamari—organic gluten-free soy sauce for the win!

• Raw organic seaweed—a great addition to a green vegetable smoothie blend.

• Sweeteners—maple syrup, dates, raw honey, and Manuka honey. We consider honey to be a superfood, but make sure it's raw and consciously harvested.

• Agar flakes—a seaweed-based thickening agent.

• Soy or sunflower lecithin—binds oils.

• Vanilla bean—this is worth spending money on.

• Maca—Mayan superfood and endurance booster. Rich loves this in his morning smoothies.

• Cacao powder and nibs—raw chocolate superfood antioxidant.

• Vegan butter—we like Earth Balance.

• Relish, pickles, and kraut—our favorite brand is Bubbies—high in amino acids!

• Fermented beet kraut—find a good brand at your farmers' market.

• Gourmet Kalamata olives—we always have these on hand for our untuna and pizza recipes.

• Apple cider vinegar—balancing with an alkalizing effect on the body. Try a tablespoon in filtered water daily in the morning.

• Balsamic vinegar—harkening Italy, it works well to sweeten a dressing, for carmelizing portobellos, or over arugula.

• High-quality BBQ sauce—we prefer Annie's.

• Vegan Worcestershire sauce—we prefer Annie's for this also.

• High-quality Italian balsamic glaze.

• Rose water—the secret ingredient in our Divine Vibration Blend (page 52).

EQUIPMENT LIST

Here are the essential tools needed for Plantpower mastery in the kitchen.*

Vitamix

The number one tool that will make creating Plantpowered recipes a breeze is the Vitamix. We use ours at least three times per day. We also travel with it when possible or we arrange to borrow one at our destination.

The Vitamix is a super-high-powered blender that blends up entire veggies with skins, roots, and all. It's the first thing we go to in the morning to make our Plantpowered blends. Julie also uses it for quick raw tomato sauces, nut cheeses, ice creams, soups, gravies, pesto, chocolate shakes, and raw cookies.

You will fall in love with your Vitamix. There are now five different models. To start, you only need the beginner model. If you can afford it, get one with variable speed. And only if you are a seasoned chef or caterer do you need the highest-powered model. Vitamix also offers reduced-price refurbished models for the more budget-conscious consumer.

Masticating Juicer

This machine is the latest evolution in juicing and we love it. It is a slower, gentler process that masticates, or "chews," the ingredients. This preserves the life force, or prana, of the fruits and veggies. We highly recommend this machine (Omega makes a fantastic variety—omegajuicers.com) for juicing as our life force and vital energy are integral components to increased health and wellness.

Food Processor

A great food processor is also one of the pillars of kitchen equipment that will serve you well in preparing Plantpowered meals. If you get a large Cuisinart, it will last you for many, many years. We don't recommend the smaller ones unless you live alone. The bowl just doesn't hold enough volume to be efficient. Julie uses the food processor for making walnut untuna, pie crusts, walnut Parmesan cheese, and salsas. It processes less than the Vitamix, so you can pulse for varied textures in recipes. We use this machine every three days or so.

Wok

We love using a wok to blacken certain veggies for flavor. It distributes the heat very evenly and its larger volume allows us to get a lot done quickly. We try not to cook our food too long; using a wok or cast-iron skillet gives a quick blast of heat so that you can get a cooked surface and keep the inside juicy. They last forever, so they are a great purchase.

Knives

We like to work with three or four different knives. Julie likes a serrated knife, large and medium chopping knives, and a smaller paring knife. Knives are personal to each chef. We don't recommend buying the huge block that sits on the counter, as it's overkill. We aren't cutting steak! Just choose three good knives that feel nice in your hand and keep them sharp. That is all you will ever need.

---

* Note: We have not been sponsored, paid, or in any way financially incentivized to endorse or promote any of the products recommended in this section or anywhere else in this book (other than our own products). This is just the stuff we like, plain and simple.

Mandoline

This is a super-handy tool for cutting zucchini into lasagna-noodle thickness. We didn't have it in the early days, and my sons and Julie have cut many a zucchini by hand, but having this mandoline makes the process so much faster. Just keep this away from little ones. The blade is very sharp. Be careful not to cut yourself. Make sure to buy a model with a hand guard and always wear a protective glove during use.

Spiral Slicer

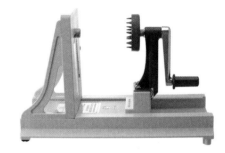

These are great for making veggie spaghetti out of squash or zucchini. You can also add spiraled beets or carrots to salads. Our girls love helping and it's well worth the investment.

Springform Pans

We love these pans! Having springform pans will make you into a formidable pastry chef and your pies will impress and delight! Making raw pies is the easiest thing ever! We prefer a 12" pan.

Cutting Boards

Plastic cutting boards are light and easy sheets you can cut on. If you have little ones, they can carry them with ease. You can't beat the price and functionality. If you want a more substantial cutting board, a good marble cutting board is a worthwhile investment. We use ours to serve custom cakes or spreads of fruits and veggies. These will last you for years. And for sustainable wood, bamboo cutting boards are perfect.

Nut Milk Bag

You can find one for ten dollars at a specialty natural foods market. It will make your nut milk prep a breeze.

Mason Jars

Keeping your nuts, seeds, and dry goods fresh will be easy in mason jars. They also keep your pantry orderly—and it's easier to be inspired when you can quickly identify what ingredients you have to work with. Get a couple of cases. You can also drink your blends out of these and take them on the road to work with you, which will support you in living Plantpowered.

Mixing Bowls

Glass bowls are great for mixing and for sauces. Our favorite mixing bowls come with lids so you can store your sauces or leftovers in glass, which we prefer over plastic.

Pots and Pans

Copper is the best conductor of heat. If you want pans that will last a lifetime, these are your best bet. They have stainless-steel interiors, so they are nontoxic.

Lasagna Pan

Having a large rectangular pan for building vegan lasagna or baking brownies is a must.

Large Steamer Pot with Strainer

This is one item that Julie uses almost daily. Our favorite is stainless steel and has two strainers, which make it really versatile and highly functional.

Coco Jack

This is a handy and super-efficient tool that will support you in opening young coconuts safely. The jack has proven to be an invaluable tool for our family. For opening brown coconuts, we recommend researching safe techniques online. For more information, instructional videos, and to purchase, visit coco-jack.com.

KALELUJAH!

I entered into this world of cooking and creating food from a purely authentic desire to cook great healthy food for my ultra-athlete husband and four children.

In 2008, Rich began to chase a dream. In preparation for his first Ultraman World Championship, he was training crazy hours (upwards of thirty hours per week). As he would kiss me good-bye and set out for a ten-hour training ride, I vividly recall asking myself, *What can I possibly feed him when he arrives home, depleted and starved? What would truly serve his body and promote optimum recovery?* I wanted to support him both nutritionally and energetically. And so I began experimenting with plant-based whole foods to create dishes both healthy and satisfying. As I progressed, inspirations dropped in and meals emerged. He was grateful for the care, enjoying the taste as well as the energetic nutritional boost. Soon, I started asking the children to weigh in on their favorite dishes. *What do you think of this almond pesto? How was the date nut crust on this pie? What about the cacao tomato sauce? What do you think we should have for dinner tonight?* Cooking is collaborative. It's experiential. It's artistic. And in our case, it's the very fabric and foundation of our family lifestyle. Since 2008, we have never stopped creating—compiling new recipes and refining favorites with improvements in preparation and augmented nutrition. Meanwhile, we never tire of researching the latest in health science and are always on the lookout for new methods and foods to optimally support our body, mind, and spirit. This process is both evolutionary and revolutionary. Now more than seven years into this journey, we are beyond proud to finally and joyfully present the best of our evolution in the plant-based whole-food recipes in this beautiful cookbook.

On any world-famous culinary school's scale of preparation difficulty, every single recipe in this book would be considered beyond simplistic. And any well-trained chef would be unimpressed by my rudimentary technique. The truth is, I have no formal training. I lack chopping finesse. Instead, I make up my own rules, relying on gut creative instincts, a willingness to be bold in the kitchen, and a devotion to persistently experiment. Don't get me wrong, I am well aware that I could gain much from attending culinary school, and I still might just sign up!

Here's a funny story to illustrate. A couple of years ago, a Michelin restaurant-trained chef signed up to attend one of my cooking workshops. As I showered on the morning of the event, I wondered, *Why on earth is this educated chef coming to **my** class?* I just couldn't figure it out. A generous spirit, he turned out to be wonderfully open and curious. To my great surprise, he really enjoyed observing my creativity in action. But when he asked me, "Why did you select that knife to chop the zucchini?" I could only answer, "Because this was the one closest to me?"

Is that a valid answer? Actually, being a wife, author, musician, healer, and mother of four, time is extremely precious. I am constantly searching for ways I can simplify my life. So in answer to this question, I say a triumphant YES!

I share this experience with you so you understand that I am just like you—simply a person who wants to prepare and enjoy delicious healthy food with my family. I may not have technique or a fancy culinary degree, but I enter into food preparation and recipe creation from a place of feeling. I have a very deep and pure desire to infuse love, celebration, and healing into my family and anyone who eats my food. *Isn't that what we all truly want?* Mother Nature has already done all the hard work. Much of what I do is move out of the way and allow her to inspire me through the beautiful foods she provides. I simply feature the inherent tastes, colors, and aromas of plant-based whole foods that were designed for us to not just exist but thrive. If I have any specialty at all, it's my ability to create freely and spontaneously. The touch to transform simple natural foods into authentic creations that are beautiful, unique, and elegant.

How much time will it take you to prepare plant-based recipes? That depends on how fast you chop! Preparation times for recipes in this book range from ten minutes to one hour. On the outside range, for a larger group, you may have a meal that takes perhaps one and a half hours. But most dishes in this book can be prepared in thirty minutes or less—arguably less time than it would take you to drive for takeout. The kitchen time is definitely better spent because the quality of what you will be putting in your body (nutrients, taste, energy, and intentions) will far surpass anything you could possibly get via takeout. I approach cooking as an artistic expression. My preparations are spontaneous and creatively inspired, such that no two meals can ever be the same. How could they be? You are a different person in each moment! Each time you prepare a recipe, you bring unique energy to the process, which inevitably alters the result. Holding this perspective gives space for great freedom. Freedom for new and

unique experiences. And most important, freedom from mistakes. Because in creativity, there are no mistakes—only new ways of creating. Take a moment and ponder the concept. Feeling relieved? You've got this!

I feel that anyone, experienced or novice, can immediately utilize any of these recipes and have a great meal on the table in no time.

There are few things more powerful than a great meal that feeds the body and soul. Intimidated by such a tall order? Don't be. Superb food is far more about intention and fresh ingredients than it is about preparation minutiae. So I invite you to let go of your kitchen fears. Release your trepidation about the process, execution, and result of your attempts. All that energy is better spent on loving thoughts for yourself and your family. My point? Simply give yourself permission to begin the journey. You're ready. And we have been waiting for you with open arms. I want you to remember along the way that I believe in you and I trust you to find your true home, the place where you are eating to thrive and loving it. Thank you for meeting us here. We are blessed to join you around this sacred table of life, sharing such beautiful food and experiences of living a plant-based lifestyle.

May we all continue to experience the expansion inherent in living Plantpowered!

BLENDS +
JUICES

TO BLEND OR TO JUICE...

A juice or a blend? A blend or a juice? So many people want the answer to this burning question. Our answer is always the same: *it depends*. A better question we could ask is, *for whom and when?*

Think of juice like medicine. When we talk about juice we're not talking about store-bought OJ. Instead, we're talking about organic, freshly prepared, and slowly masticated vegetables, fruits, and roots. In the most general sense, juicing removes the food's pulpy fiber, leaving only the water and most of the nutrients to enjoy. Prepared this way, juice truly can be medicinal. Removing the fiber expedites nutrient absorption. So juicing is like mainlining a highly concentrated mega-dose of phytonutrients, micronutrients, antioxidants, minerals, and vitamins straight into your bloodstream.

Think of blends as a meal. By contrast, blending does not remove the pulpy fiber, pulverizing the fruit, vegetables, nuts, and/ or seeds (depending upon what you are blending, of course) to produce a more robust, calorically and nutritionally dense smoothie concoction of compacted nutrients. Think of blends as partially pre-digested meals served up for maximum net nutrient gain since you can digest them easily. Plus the added fiber (extracted in juicing) is important. It aids in digestive health and moderates blood glucose levels by slowing down the absorption of sugar.

Long story short? We love both. And both have their place in a Plantpowered lifestyle.

Vitality & Energy

Irrespective of dietary proclivities, it's no mystery that everyone can benefit from eating more whole fruits and vegetables. If you are looking to increase your energy and vitality, starting your morning with a juice or a blend is a great way to boost your micronutrient intake and kick-start your day feeling great.

Pro tip: Make sure you vary your recipes to allow for the greatest range of nutrients.

Newbies & Weight Loss

If you are new to eating lots of veggies, trying to lose a few extra pounds, or want to clear some processed foods from your digestive tract, you are going to want to start introducing a rotation of vegetable-based green juices into your daily food intake.

You will likely benefit from introducing some vegetable-based blends into your diet as well. But it's important to be wary of unwanted extra calories. You'd be surprised how easy it is to pack a tremendous caloric load into a blend and dupe yourself into thinking you are eating well, only to find out that your morning smoothie is calorically akin to a chocolate milk shake.

Pro tip: The foundation of your blend should always be dark leafy greens like kale and spinach. Keep your smoothies predominantly vegetable-based. Avoid nuts, nut milks, oils (like hemp and flax), and avocados. Limit added fruit and forget about adding fruit juice—opt for filtered water instead.

Athletic Performance & Recovery

Preworkout, keep it relatively light. A simple green juice is great or a light blend of kale, spirulina, pineapple, and hemp seeds will hit the spot and get you out the door for that early-morning training session.

Post-workout, it's important to get a recovery blend high in protein, electrolytes, and glycogen into your system within thirty minutes of your training session. This will expedite muscular repair, replenish your energy stores, combat free radical damage, and balance your equilibrium. Making this a priority is the key to bouncing back quickly so you can get the most out of your training day after day. Rich is living proof—his blends keep him fueled and feeling great even during his most intensive training blocks.

Pro tip: When motivation wanes, a fortified green juice could be just the inspiration you need to hop on your bike or hit the gym. If you can get a fresh juice in mid-ride, you'll be smiling.

Juicing Tips

Again, juicing is a great way to get concentrated nutrients into your system quickly. We utilize juicing in a variety of ways. Juicing in the early morning during the hotter months is a great way to embrace a summer dawn. Feel a cold coming on during the winter months? A shot of fresh turmeric-ginger juice will keep the doctor away. Simply put, there is nothing that makes the body feel better than a fresh organic green juice. So have fun experimenting with combinations of kale, celery, cucumber, herbs, and spinach.

Try to keep your juices predominantly vegetable-based, limiting fruit, raw beets, and carrots. These foods are loaded with sugar, which causes your insulin to spike, followed by a blood sugar crash. Vibrant health and longevity requires balancing your blood sugar and insulin levels. If you want to include carrots or beets in your juices, try steaming them first and always use in moderation.

Pro tip: If you are feeling hard-core, consider adopting a periodic one-day vegetable juice fast throughout the year. It's a great way to give your digestive system a break. Sometimes a mini three-day juice fast once per season is just the thing to reboot the system.

Blending Tips

There are only so many plants you can juice. But the sky is the limit when it comes to blends. Using the recipes in this book as a general guide, we encourage you to experiment with combinations of greens like kale and spinach. Sprouts like alfalfa and broccoli. Vegetables like beet, carrot, and bell pepper. Seeds like hemp, chia, and ground flax. Nuts like raw almonds, walnuts, and cashews. And superfoods like maca, spirulina, and chlorella. Plant-based milk varieties with fruits like banana and pineapple make for frothy delicious additions to any meal or that can be a healthy dessert option.

Again, be mindful of the amount of sugary fruits in your blends. The added fiber will slow down the absorption of sugar in your system somewhat, but you'll still experience an insulin spike. Therefore, and as a rule of thumb, always prioritize vegetables as your primary smoothie base.

For obvious reasons, the more you pack into your blender, the thicker the smoothie. Don't overdo it. Add extra filtered water to thin out the consistency. And just because you made an entire blender full doesn't mean you have to drink the entire thing!

Pro tip: Get used to drinking one robust glass of "salad" for breakfast. Pour the remaining contents of your blender into a thermos. Take it with you to sip throughout the day to stave off cravings and keep your energy levels high.

4

TRIPLE B BLEND

Bursting with berries, beets, and basil, this antioxidant-rich smoothie is packed with the power of raw plants. There is something incredibly refreshing about basil paired with blueberries. Energizing and activating, this summertime blend overflows with fiber, vitamins, iron-rich seeds, and the reparative oomph of blueberries—essential for a healthy body. Whip up this Triple B Blend and Be Well!

Ingredients

- 2 cups apple juice
- 2 cups filtered water
- 2 leaves curly kale, stripped from stalks
- Handful raw pepitas (about 2 tablespoons)
- 1½ cups frozen blueberries
- 1 banana
- ½" piece fresh ginger with skin
- ½" slice raw beet with skin
- 8 basil leaves, stems removed
- ½ lemon, peeled

Preparation

In a Vitamix or high-powered blender, add all the ingredients; blend on high for a minute. Drink!

CHERRY CACAO BLEND

Almost too good to be true, this frozen chocolate cherry shake will make you smile. Filled with real fruits, cacao, superfood seeds, and a pinch of kale, this energizing delight will celebrate your body. Cherries are high in B vitamins, such as thiamin, riboflavin, and vitamin B_6—crucial for optimizing metabolism and converting nutrients into energy. Loudly slurp this blend into your tummy and feel alive.

Ingredients

- 2 cups frozen cherries
- 1 frozen banana
- 2 tablespoons cacao powder
- 2 tablespoons chia seeds
- 2 tablespoons cacao nibs
- 1 leaf dinosaur kale
- 1 cup apple juice
- 1 cup filtered water

Preparation

In a Vitamix or high-powered blender, add all the ingredients; blend on high for a minute. Drink!

DEEP BLUE SEA BLEND

Hawaii in a glass. When Rich raced the Ultraman World Championship on the Big Island of Hawaii, we experienced the beautiful island spirit of *kokua*, extending love to others, and *ohana*, or family. This blend is a little gift of *kokua* to our Plantpowered *ohana*. Brimming with manganese, thiamin, and vitamin C, this sweet, tropical island elixir supports a healthy immune system. Spirulina delivers the ocean within by providing potent detoxifying properties, phytonutrients, and a high level of protein from the sea. Drink this blend and immerse yourself in the healing aqua waters of Hawaii. Aloha!

Ingredients

- 2 cups chopped pineapple
- 1 frozen banana
- ½ cup raw coconut
- 4 cups coconut water
- ½ teaspoon spirulina

Preparation

In a Vitamix or high-powered blender, add all the ingredients; blend on high for a minute. Drink!

GREEN EXTREME BLEND

Every so often, we crave a large super-green veggie blend to turbocharge the day. This thick, lively concoction is full of exciting flavors. A powerhouse combination where greens, herbs, seeds, and superfoods unite to form a salty, lemony, and spicy vitamin K–infused rocket fuel. Get ready for orbit after ingesting this power drink. But buyer beware: you might just find yourself signing up for an ultramarathon or writing your first book. When in doubt, this blend is your go-to option. Drink responsibly!

Ingredients

- ½ avocado
- 8 pitted Kalamata olives
- ½ jalapeño
- Juice of 2 lemons
- 5 sprigs fresh cilantro
- 4 large basil leaves
- ¼ cup raw pumpkin seeds
- 1 tablespoon ground flaxseeds
- 1 tablespoon hemp seeds
- 2 celery stalks
- ¼ cup dried seaweed
- 2 large leaves dinosaur kale
- 1 cup filtered water
- 1 teaspoon Celtic sea salt
- Ice

Preparation

1. Remove the pit and skin from the avocado half.

2. Add all the ingredients except the ice into a Vitamix or high-powered blender. Process for a full minute. Adjust the taste by adding more lemon juice, olives, or seaweed. Add ice and process for another 30 seconds. Enjoy!

Chef's Note: This blend makes a great soup! Omit the ice and keep blending for a full 4 minutes and you'll have a warm elixir to complement your lunch.

KIDS' MANGO BLEND

This is a perfect recipe featuring the beloved fruit of children everywhere: mango! There is nothing quite like this sweet yet aromatic fruit. Let the potassium balance your electrolytes and help control heart rate and blood pressure. The sweet flavors in this smoothie mask the nutritional yeast, which provides a healthy dose of vitamin B_{12}, a crucial nutrient for every Plantpowered body. Blend this smoothie up and watch your kids ask for more.

Ingredients

- 2 bananas
- 1 cup frozen mango
- 1 cup frozen strawberries
- Handful fresh sprouts, or 1 kale leaf
- 1 tablespoon nutritional yeast
- 1½ cups coconut water or filtered water

Preparation

Throw everything into a Vitamix or high-powered blender and blend for a full minute.

Chef's Note: When preparing blends for children, always throw in a teaspoon of nutritional yeast or a handful of greens or fresh sprouts. It's a great way to get more greens into their growing bodies!

DIVINE VIBRATION BLEND

After my morning meditation I often cut roses and gather herbs from our garden to put into my morning blend. Using fresh flower petals connects me to nature, infusing my body and soul with the wisdom and grace of great feminine power. Man or woman, I feel we can all use a little more divine mother energy in our lives, don't you think? This orange-based blend combined with carrot, lemon, lavender, sage, and rose is a soulful, spiritual elixir that will set your day on a positive trajectory of empowerment.

Ingredients

- 1 cup coconut water
- 1 organic sweet grapefruit
- 1 organic carrot
- 1 organic lemon, peeled
- 3 fresh red or pink rose petals
- 4 fresh white sage leaves
- 1 stalk aloe vera fillet, skin removed
- 3 fresh lavender blooms, from your garden or local farmer's market
- 1 teaspoon rose water
- 1 cup ice (optional)

Preparation

Throw everything except the ice into the Vitamix or high-powered blender and blend for a full minute. Add the ice, if desired.

MONK BLEND

Designed for your spiritual mountain trek, this blend is a fresh twist on a traditional mango lassi. Packed with fiber, antioxidants, anti-inflammatory turmeric, almonds, and vitamins A and C, this blend delivers the luscious, creamy consistency of your dream superfood shake. Goji berries, an ancient Himalayan superfood, promote strength, longevity, and divinity of mind. Let the expansive energy of this blend connect you to your higher self. Sip it mindfully. Namaste!

Ingredients

• Handful fresh goji berries, or ¼ cup dried goji berries, soaked for 30 minutes or more

• ½" piece fresh turmeric root, peeled

• 1" piece fresh ginger, peeled

• 1 large orange, peeled

• 1 cup frozen mango

• Handful raw almonds, soaked for 30 minutes or overnight

• 1 cup orange juice

• 1 cup filtered water

Preparation

Throw everything into the Vitamix or high-powered blender and blend for a full minute.

ULTRA QUEEN K PERFORMANCE BLEND

The pure raw energy of this blend works like magic to provide the energy you need to power through your most challenging workout. Blends like this one have served as crucial support throughout Rich's ultra-endurance training and racing. A trifecta of chia, flax, and hemp seeds works together to provide protein, omega-3 fats, and fiber to keep your motor fortified and supercharged for hours. Sweet pineapple and dates mean this blend is bursting with energy. Embrace your inner superhero and allow your best, most authentic self to emerge!

Ingredients

- 1 cup pineapple, skin removed
- 4 large leaves dinosaur kale
- 1 teaspoon maca powder
- 2 tablespoons chia seeds
- 2 teaspoons ground flaxseeds
- 2 tablespoons hemp seeds
- ½ cup raw coconut
- 2 tablespoons coconut oil
- 3 dates, pitted
- 1 teaspoon blue-green algae
- 3 cups filtered water

Preparation

In a Vitamix or high-powered blender, add all the ingredients; blend on high for a minute. Drink!

EPIC5 RECOVERY BLEND

Recovery blends are a key piece in every athlete's training program. This blend is formulated in the spirit of EPIC5, Rich's adventure completing five ironman-distance triathlons on five Hawaiian Islands in less than a week. Reparative nourishment after a long training session is essential to success. Here's one of Rich's go-to blends after a long ride. Power packed with plants, seeds, protein, and superfood galore, it's certain to recharge and repair, no matter how hard you push yourself. Not for the faint of heart!

Ingredients

- 2 kale leaves
- ½ small beet with its greens
- 1 apple (red, pink, or green local variety), cored
- 1 cup fresh or frozen blueberries
- 1 tablespoon acai powder
- 1 teaspoon maca powder
- ¼ cup pumpkin seeds
- 1 teaspoon spirulina
- 1 scoop Rich Roll's REPAIR Protein Supplement or favorite protein supplement
- 1 tablespoon hemp seeds
- ¼ cup goji berries
- 3 cups coconut water or filtered water

Preparation

In a Vitamix or high-powered blender, add all the ingredients; blend on high for a minute. Drink!

Chef's Note: One reality of living with four children is that we never quite know what we have in the fridge on any given day. So more often than not, Rich will improvise when making this blend, based on supplies. Use as many dark leafy greens as you can and don't sweat the details if you don't have every one of these ingredients in your pantry.

JUICES

To get you started, here's a three-ingredient juice recipe template to keep things simple, refreshing, and delicious. These are some of our family favorites. But don't stop here. Go wild experimenting with your favorite fruits and veggies and come up with your own creative combinations. There are no limits! Please make certain that all juicing ingredients are organic.

Carrot Ginger Aloe

Antioxidant, digestive, soothing. Great when you feel a cold coming on.

Ingredients

- 3 carrots
- 1" piece fresh ginger, peeled
- 2" piece aloe

Beet Parsley Apple

Blood fortifying, vitamin K, energizing. A great preworkout boost.

Ingredients

- 1 beet
- 1 bunch fresh parsley
- 1 apple (red, pink, or green local variety)

Dandelion Lemon Celery

Alkalizing, vitamin K shot, cleansing. Great to reboot the system.

Ingredients

- 4 dandelion leaves
- 1 large lemon
- 2 celery stalks

Cucumber Lemon Cilantro

Hydrating, alkalizing, and detoxifying.

Ingredients

- 1 cucumber
- 1 lemon
- 1 small bunch cilantro

Turmeric Orange Ginger

Super anti-inflammatory, mood lifting, and activating. A wellness powerhouse and perfect post-workout.

Ingredients

- 3" piece fresh turmeric
- 1 orange
- 1" piece fresh ginger, peeled

Pineapple Ginger Mint

Great source of vitamin C. Aids circulation and digestion.

Ingredients

- 1 cup chopped pineapple, skin removed
- 2" piece fresh ginger, peeled
- 1 bunch fresh mint

YOU KNOW WHAT TO DO . . .

BE ADVENTUROUS, GO AHEAD, EXPLORE . . .

RAISING HEALTHY KIDS WITH A PLANTPOWERED LIFESTYLE APPROACH

As parents we all want what's best for our kids, including healthy eating habits. This is a daunting prospect for many. But with patience and the right approach, it's not only possible, it's actually not that hard. Sure, it will take time. But if you consistently adhere to a few simple principles, including the tips and experience shared in this section, it won't be long before you begin to notice a positive sea change in your children's default habits around food—a priceless step in the direction of greater long-term family health.

As a whole, our society is in a pretty scary place when it comes to all the highly enticing unhealthy foods ingeniously marketed to attract the fancy of undiscerning youngsters. Just walk the aisles of a typical grocery store. All the beautiful living plant foods are relegated to a single distant corner that might as well be Siberia. By contrast, artificially enhanced, seductively packaged processed foods rife with salt, sugar, fat, chemical additives, and GMOs dominate every remaining aisle of these increasingly gigantic emporiums. The result? Healthy choices become subservient to convenience. Or as the old adage goes, *out of sight, out of mind.*

Overworked, overstressed, and out of patience, you push the grocery cart down a middle aisle as your phone rings and your youngest squeals with delight upon seeing her favorite sugary breakfast cereal. *Who has time for a nutrition lecture?* It's just easier to reflexively grab the frozen pizza, hot dogs, or the pretty box with the hypnotic, misleading label. I get it. But this conditioned response isn't just lazy, it's irresponsible, fostering a dangerous cycle of unhealthy food addiction so entrenched that when we finally offer our kids a vegetable, they look at us like we're insane.

Regrettably, most parents are thrilled if they can get their child to even look at broccoli or maybe take a bite out of the occasional carrot. Apples and grapes make the grade, provided they come in some kind of prepackaged "lunchable" product accompanied by cheese and salty crackers. The horrendous state of most school lunch programs isn't helping. Feeling helpless and fatigued, we inevitably give in, reasoning that it is better to give them pizza and chips than nothing. *I mean they have to eat something, right?*

The first step in overcoming the madness requires that we as parents step up and take responsibility for the uncomfortable truth that we have played a large part in creating and reinforcing the problem. It's our job to foster positive life habits in the young ones under our care, and this of course includes the foods we choose and prepare. So let's start taking that job more seriously. Kids inherit their behavior cues from us. *It's not what you say, it's what you do.* A crucial step in getting your kids to change their eating habits requires alignment between your words and your actions. You can't tell little Johnny to eat his spinach when he knows you hit the drive-through. You might be able to fool yourself by failing to walk your talk, but you won't fool them. Kids are incredibly intuitive!

I hate to sound so strident, but we must face the fact that childhood obesity rates and the incidence of young people with type 2 diabetes is shamefully high and skyrocketing out of control. The time was yesterday for swift, decisive action. I am sympathetic to the fact that adopting a whole-food, plant-centric approach can be intimidating, but we can no longer afford to let our personal emotional baggage interfere with the long-term welfare of our precious children.

If this book has any purpose, it's to dispel the fear you might be feeling. The important thing is to break the paralysis and just begin making better choices, one at a time. Don't think about next week's meal, only think about what you are eating and serving now. And let's not focus on the animal-based and processed foods we are removing from our diet. Instead, let's spotlight the bounty of beautiful healthy foods we are including. The simplest and single-most effective change you can make today is to start increasing the amount of daily greens in your family's meals. Forget about dogma. Let go of rules and labels. Without any grand proclamations, just quietly and gradually start adding more and more fresh produce to your children's plates (and yours). Pack your child's lunch with a banana, apple, or some raw almonds instead of cookies. Sure, they might resist at first, but kids are surprisingly adaptable. Be patient. Be consistent. What was unusual will soon become the norm.

Over time, as you and your family blaze this new path, have faith that you and your loved ones will come to intuitively understand the fundamental relationship between food choice and vitality. The desire to feel good will begin to motivate healthier choices across the board. Want to hear something really wild? Ramping up your plant intake will seed the intestinal tract with a healthier microbial ecology that will profoundly impact cravings. Soon that hankering for a cheeseburger will be replaced by a desire to eat the foods that make you feel great. I realize it sounds crazy, but it's true. It happened for us. It happened for our kids. And it can happen for your family, too.

You may be asking: how can I prepare a meal that will work for all the members of my family? Maybe you want to go plant-based but your husband is a hardened carnivore. Your daughter is lactose intolerant. Your son has a peanut allergy and won't eat anything unless it is slathered in cheese. As a mother of four, I empathize. Families are a complex composite of preferences and personalities. Indeed, it can be challenging to divine a single meal plan that makes everyone happy. I don't have the miracle answer to solve this problem for you overnight. But nothing good happens overnight anyway. Creating sustainable lifestyle change is a constantly evolving journey that takes tremendous patience, persistence, and experimentation. However, I will leave you with one non-negotiable rule—the key to meeting this challenge is ensuring that a preponderance of healthy fruits and vegetables find their way onto every family member's plate at every meal, period.

Here are some more vital tools to help you and your children make the shift:

Walk Your Talk

Again, I cannot overemphasize how important it is to lead by example. Your actions simply must line up with your words. That doesn't mean you have to be all in. But it means being honest, transparent, and accountable to your children regarding your own eating habits. Nobody is perfect, and this subject is a great platform to communicate openly with your kids about what is working for you and what is difficult. Children are smarter than we give them credit for. Honesty breeds trust. And it truly is a two-way street. Simply put, you will not win their respect if you bark at them about salad while you raid the fridge for cheesecake at midnight.

Embrace Everyone with Unconditional Love and Acceptance

It's important to meet people where they're at. We're not here to tell anyone what they should or should not do, only to share our experience and what we have learned for those who are interested. Everyone is on his or her own path. We find it best to reserve judgment and trust that every individual has a compass to guide his or her way in his or her own time. The most powerful gift you can offer your children is true love and respect. The only real goal here is to get more healthy plants into their diet. Consider every time that happens a triumph and don't focus on the negative. Keep preparing amazing food and they will come to love and even appreciate it. Don't take "I don't like it" as gospel. Try it again and again. Never give up. Just keep persisting, creating, and experimenting.

Family Time Is Sacred

You must establish the sanctity of family dinners. As much as possible, let the evening meal be one you share together. Invest the time to prepare meals together as a unit whenever possible. This is crucial to your intimate connection with your family.

Creatively Involve Your Kids in Recipe Preparation

Involving our children in the process of growing, buying, preparing, and serving food has been revolutionary. Each step in this process is an invaluable educational and experiential opportunity for your kids. Take them along with you to the market. If there is a farmers' market in your area, even better. Strike up a conversation with the farmers themselves and encourage your kids to ask questions. Engage your children in a lively, detailed discussion about why you are choosing the foods you select. Ask them which foods they would like prepared for dinner and why. Have them find recipes they like and then prepare the dishes together. Time in the kitchen with kids is valuable life experience. Teaching young kids to cook healthy dishes breeds a sense of pride, ownership, and self-esteem. The first thing we taught our little girls to make is our chia seed pudding. Because they learned how to make it and enjoyed the process, it quickly became a family favorite, supplanting all store-bought dessert options. Great recipes will become part of your family tradition. Learning how to prepare healthy food together will transform your lives.

Become a Great Cook

I truly believe that everyone is naturally creative. The kitchen is a great outlet for unique expression. Don't be intimidated by the daunting prospect of cooking for your family. It's a blessing! You don't have to be a Michelin restaurant-trained chef to roll up your sleeves and be inspired in the kitchen. Follow the recipes in this book until you get the hang of it. Then jump off into your own inspired creations! If your healthy productions taste great (and they will), your kids will beg for it.

Bring Green Drinks into Your Home

Start working green drinks into your kids' routine. If blending and juicing is a new concept for your family, ease into it with delicious fruit-based smoothies or creamy almond-and-banana varieties (they taste like milk shakes). But always slip in a leaf or two of kale. Over time, as you and your kids acclimate, begin upping the "green quotient" of your blends by adding some spinach, cucumber, celery, or chard. This is highly effective!

Prepare a Family Meal

Try not to fall into the habit of making separate "kids meals." The more often you prepare a wide assortment of vegetables, fruits, nuts, seeds, and legumes, the more range your children will start to accept. Make sure you don't use garlic or strong spices if you have little ones. Adults can always add more spice to their plate after the meal is served.

Create a Beautiful Table and Setting

Enlist your children to design a table arrangement using twigs from the garden or toys from their rooms. Make it an artful event with complete creative freedom for the kids. They will start to enjoy and look forward to eating at the table as a family. Soon, that veggie they turned up their noses at will turn up in their stomachs.

More Love

Above all, love your children unconditionally. None of this diet or lifestyle should bring any hardness or judgment into your family. Stand as an example and work on your own food issues while continuing to provide great healthy choices.

NUT MILKS, CREAMS & CHEESES

One of the most difficult ideas for most of us to get our head around when considering a Plantpowered lifestyle is the idea of giving up dairy. *How could I possibly give up cheese? How will I survive without milk in my lattes?* I was certain that I couldn't.

It seems nearly impossible that one could actually enjoy life without these creamy pleasures. But the stone-cold truth is that dairy consumption is making us sick. This product of horribly mistreated and reprehensibly overmedicated animals fattened with genetically modified grain and brimming with injected hormones finds its way into our milks, cheeses, yogurts, and ice creams. Dairy is linked to the onset of heart disease, digestive disorders, osteoporosis *(the irony!)*, early-onset puberty, and even cancer. These grim downsides make dairy consumption non-negotiable for the discerning health-conscious consumer.

So what now?

Granted, the leap to give up dairy is one tough ask. But you are fraught for naught because the "creamy" you will discover in nature's nuts and fruits goes far beyond anything you've ever tasted from a goat or cow.

First of all, you fall in *love* with the taste. Then your skin miraculously clears up. Persistent sinus congestion? Gone. Those pesky last few pounds around the waist you just can't seem to lose no matter what? Suddenly they are melting away. Arterial health and digestion improve. And chronic allergies fade to distant memories. Before you know it, you are more energetic than you have been in years.

That, dear friends, is what happens when you part ways with dairy and embrace a plant-based approach that includes the rich and creamy, full-bodied, protein-filled, nourishing milks, creams, cheeses, and ice creams you thought all vegans were missing out on.

The variety of creamy, cheesy options that can be created with nuts is just incredible. To that we say, "Thank you, Mother Nature!" Making your own is a must. It's just so easy! The flavor and freshness far surpass any store-bought nut milks, many of which contain extra sugar and additives you simply don't need. We like to use cashews, Brazil nuts, and macadamia nuts in our cheese varieties. Almonds, walnuts, cashews, and hemp seeds make up our favorite varieties of milks, occasionally sweetened with fresh dates.

For creamy cheese sauce, we use nuts plus quantities of nutritional yeast, chickpea, rice, or soy miso paste with lemon, water, and garlic. When you heat the nut sauce on the stove, it will thicken very quickly. As you get acclimated, you can even experiment by adding herbs and veggies to your cheese varieties.

Coconut milks and raw coconut provide the base for many of our ice creams and frozen superfood pies. The best part of all of this? It takes almost no time and little effort to whip up your own cheesy sauce to pour over Torre de Nachos (page 207). *The milkman never delivered a better glass of cold milk than the one you'll be making.* And before you know it, you'll be a pie chef, too!

Here it is, milk that actually **does** do your body good. Bam!

HEMP MILK

This is hands down my favorite milk. Shall I count the reasons why I worship the tiny, potent hemp seed? It's not why you think. They won't get you high, but they are high in nutrients. Containing all the essential amino acids, they are rich in protein as well as those important fatty acids. Easy to prepare, they don't have to be soaked overnight, nor do they require straining after I whip them into a frothy milk. But I think the main reason I love them so has to do with ease of digestion. This milk floats through my system like a fairy godmother making all my dreams come true.

Ingredients

- ¼ cup hemp seeds
- 2 cups filtered water

Preparation

In a Vitamix or high-powered blender, add the seeds and water. Blend on high for 30 seconds to 1 minute. Pour into a mason jar or right into your glass. *That's it? Yes, that's it. Boom.*

WHITE SESAME SEED MILK

A great alternative to nuts, sesame seeds make a light frothy milk that is great for adding a bit of "creamy" into your life. Sesame seeds are very low in cholesterol and sodium. They are also great sources of calcium, iron, and magnesium. This milk can be a bit bitter for some, so I always add a date and some vanilla bean. *Open sesame!*

Ingredients

- ¼ cup white sesame seeds
- 1 date, pitted
- ½ teaspoon vanilla extract
- 2 cups filtered water

Preparation

In a Vitamix or high-powered blender, add the seeds, date, vanilla, and water. Blend on high for 30 seconds. Pour into a mason jar and serve.

Chef's Note: If you are allergic to peanuts and tree nuts, you may also be allergic to sesame seeds. Make sure you check with your doctor.

SUNFLOWER SEED MILK

This seed milk embodies the beautiful yellow bloom of the beloved sunflower. I make sure this fresh milk is a regular in our family rotation. The bright taste reminds me of the vast sunflower fields that grace the Tuscan hills of Italy. Sunflowers are a wonderful metaphor for our Plantpowered tribe—a thriving global community of individual souls reaching for the sun as one.

Ingredients

- ¼ cup sunflower seeds, shelled
- Pinch Celtic sea salt
- 2 cups filtered water

Preparation

1. To a Vitamix or high-powered blender, add the seeds, salt, and water. Blend on high for 30 seconds.

2. Strain through a fine-mesh strainer or cheesecloth (optional).

3. Pour into a mason jar and serve.

CASHEW MILK

This nut milk has a creamy, thick quality I adore. Cashews are prolific healers in the plant kingdom. Classified as good fats for heart health, cashews can actually lower blood pressure and cholesterol. They are also high in iron, selenium, zinc, and magnesium. A great recovery drink after a long workout! Make sure you first soak your cashews overnight in filtered water with a teaspoon of sea salt.

Ingredients

- ¼ cup raw cashews, soaked
- 2 cups filtered water

Preparation

To a Vitamix or high-powered blender, add the cashews and water. Blend on high for 1 minute. You can strain your cashew milk through some cheesecloth or a strainer. Sometimes I skip this step, as I enjoy the tiny bits of cashews in my milk. Pour into a mason jar and serve.

COCONUT MILK

The milk of the great Mother Earth, coconut milk is a nectar to be worshipped. If you invest in a handy tool to assist you in safely and easily opening raw coconuts (see page 35), you will never again settle for packaged coconut milk.

Ingredients

- 1 large coconut

Preparation

1. Over a bowl, break the coconut open carefully and safely. Reserving the liquid, scrape out the meat.

2. Place the liquid and meat into a Vitamix or high-powered blender. Blend on high for a full 2 minutes or until you have a frothy coconut milk.

3. Strain through cheesecloth or a strainer. Keep the pulp for smoothies, raw pies, or to mix into soups. Store the pulp in the refrigerator for a week or in the freezer for a month.

Chef's Note: For a great glass of chocolate milk, add 1 tablespoon raw cacao powder plus 1 date.

SWEET VANILLA ALMOND MILK

Sweet, creamy, nutty flavors combine to form a beautiful, high-nutrition nectar. Use a great-quality vanilla bean and you will taste the difference. Soaking your almonds overnight yields such great rewards in the morning. Almonds not only provide a better glass of milk than the milkman could ever deliver, but they give your body a dose of heart-healthy fats and nutrients including vitamin E, phosphorus, riboflavin, and protein. This glass of milk is pure divine.

Ingredients

- 2 cups filtered water, plus more for soaking the almonds and dates
- ½ cup raw almonds
- 3 dates
- 2" piece vanilla bean
- Pinch Celtic sea salt

Preparation

1. In filtered water, soak the almonds overnight or for at least 2 hours. In a separate bowl, soak the dates for at least 30 minutes.

2. Drain the water from the almonds and place them in the Vitamix or high-powered blender.

3. Drain the dates, remove and discard the pits, and throw the dates in with the almonds.

4. Add the 2 cups filtered water.

5. Blend on high for 1 minute.

6. Slice open the vanilla bean lengthwise and scrape out the insides. Add the scraped seeds to the date mixture. Add the sea salt. Blend again on high for 30 seconds.

7. Pour through cheesecloth or a strainer into a glass bottle.

8. Reserve the pulp and freeze for later use in baked goods or blends.

Enjoy!

CASHEW CHEESE

Here's to a healthier way to satisfy your cheese cravings. Cashews are rich in essential minerals like iron, copper, zinc, manganese, and selenium and provide a mildly sweet cheese flavor. Using chickpea miso raises the vibrational experience, but if you can't find it, use fresh non-GMO soy miso instead. When preparing, I tend to warm it in a small saucepan on the stovetop. Maybe it's because I enjoy putting my energy back into this magical dish as I gaze into the creamy sauce and envision our lives fulfilled in beauty and grace. Thoughts are things. Energy does make a difference. Infuse your sauce with the positive life experiences your heart longs for. Intend healing, love, creativity, and vibrant health for you and your family. There you have it—food as medicine.

Ingredients

- 1 cup raw cashews, soaked
- Celtic sea salt, to taste
- 2 tablespoons nutritional yeast
- ½ cup filtered water, plus more as needed
- ¼ cup chickpea or yellow soy miso
- 1 teaspoon lemon juice

Preparation

1. In a Vitamix or high-powered bender, add the cashews, sea salt, nutritional yeast, filtered water, lemon juice, and chickpea (or yellow soy) miso. Blend until smooth, adding more water if you desire a thinner consistency.

2. Transfer to a small saucepan and heat on low until warm. It will thicken up quickly. Add a small amount of water and keep stirring to achieve the desired consistency.

Chef's Note: For a green version, add 1½ cloves garlic plus 1 bunch cilantro (including the stems) and an extra tablespoon lemon juice. Blend until smooth. You may need to stop a few times and redistribute the ingredients. Add small increments of water to reach the desired consistency. Process on high for a full 3 minutes and you'll have a warm creamy cheese sauce.

TURMERIC BASIL MACADAMIA NUT CHEESE

This is a hard block cheese that you can slice and eat with fresh ripe pears or alongside our Parisian Asparagus Salad Oo La La... (page 170). Perfect for a picnic or just to have on hand in the fridge. No store-bought vegan cheese will taste as good as the one you make at home. There you have it—*fromage!*

Ingredients

- 2½ cups macadamia nuts or Brazil nuts
- 3 cups filtered water, plus more for soaking the nuts
- 2 tablespoons nutritional yeast
- 1 large garlic clove
- 1 teaspoon Celtic sea salt
- ½ teaspoon cracked black pepper
- 1 cup agar flakes
- ¼ cup plus 1 tablespoon grape seed oil
- 6 basil leaves
- 1 tablespoon grated fresh turmeric root
- 2 tablespoons chickpea miso
- 1 tablespoon lemon juice

Preparation

1. In a medium bowl, soak the nuts in filtered water overnight or for a minimum of 2 hours. Drain them.

2. In a food processor, pulse 2 cups of the nuts and the nutritional yeast until mealy in texture.

3. Add the garlic, sea salt, and pepper to the food processor and pulse three times to incorporate.

4. In a Vitamix or high-powered blender, add the remaining ½ cup nuts plus the 3 cups filtered water. Blend on high for a full minute. Pour through a strainer or cheesecloth. This will yield about 4 cups milk.

5. In a medium saucepan, add the fresh nut milk. Warm the milk, stirring in the agar flakes and ¼ cup of the grape seed oil. Continue stirring until the liquid is warm and begins to thicken a bit.

6. With the motor running, pour the warm milk into the food processor. Add the basil, turmeric, miso, and lemon juice. Continue processing until the mixture is smooth.

7. Lightly oil a glass pie pan with the remaining 1 tablespoon grape seed oil.

8. Pour the warm cheese mixture into the pan and let it cool. The cheese will start to set up quickly. Let cool completely before transferring to the refrigerator to harden.

9. After a few hours in the fridge, the cheese can be cut into wedges from your pie pan and wrapped individually in waxed paper.

CRUMBLED WALNUT PARMESAN

A more-than-adequate substitute for its dairy-based counterpart. Sprinkle this hearty nut cheese over our Gluten-Free Spaghetti di Pesto (page 220), Fettuccini Alfredo (page 227), Caesar Salad Dressing (page 111), or Portabella Parmesana (page 205). You can store this in a mason jar in the refrigerator for three days.

Ingredients

- 1 cup raw walnuts
- 2 tablespoons nutritional yeast
- 1 garlic clove
- ½ teaspoon Celtic sea salt

Preparation

1. In a food processor, pulse the walnuts until mealy in texture.

2. Add the nutritional yeast, garlic, and sea salt. Pulse again a few times to mix well.

BRAZIL NUT CREAM SPREAD

A creamy spread that inspires the passion of Brazil, these buttery, full-bodied nuts are high in magnesium. Brazil nuts are also loaded with nutrients such as potassium, calcium, iron, and selenium. They also boost testosterone. Be mindful that they contain the highest fat content of all nuts, so make this cheese for a special treat, and although you'll be tempted, don't eat more than your share. We adore this cream in our Hash Browns Tower (page 125). It also makes a tasty spread in a sandwich or on your favorite gluten-free toast.

Ingredients

- 1 cup Brazil nuts
- 2 tablespoons filtered water, plus more for soaking the nuts
- 1 garlic clove
- 1 tablespoon soy lecithin
- 1 tablespoon grape seed oil
- ⅛ teaspoon cracked black pepper
- 1 teaspoon Celtic sea salt

Preparation

1. In a small bowl, soak the Brazil nuts overnight in filtered water.

2. Drain the water from the nuts.

3. To a Vitamix or high-powered blender, add all the ingredients and the 2 tablespoons filtered water and process on high for a full minute. Transfer to a small bowl and chill for an hour.

COCONUT HONEY CREAM

Few things in creation match the light delicacy of freshly pureed coconut. This recipe is exactly like the one for coconut milk only it uses less water.

Ingredients

- 1 large fresh coconut
- 2 tablespoons raw honey

Preparation

Over a bowl, break the coconut open carefully and safely. Reserve the liquid and scoop out the coconut meat. Place the meat into the Vitamix or high-powered blender, add ¼ cup of the coconut water plus the honey, and blend for 30 seconds. Add small increments of the remaining coconut water until it reaches your desired consistency of creaminess.

CASHEW VANILLA CREAM

This cream is an irresistible topping for fresh fruit, frozen pies, or our Chia Seed Pudding (page 138). It's super easy to make and adds a little extra decadence to our dessert creations. You'll wonder why you ever thought you needed dairy in the first place!

Ingredients

- 1 cup raw cashews, soaked
- ½ cup raw honey
- 2 teaspoons vanilla extract
- 2 tablespoons soy lecithin
- ¼ cup filtered water, plus move as needed

Preparation

1. In a Vitamix or high-powered blender, add all the ingredients and blend on high for a full minute. Adjust the thickness by adding more water.

2. Transfer to a serving bowl and refrigerate. This will cause the cream to thicken.

Alternatively, you can pour the cream on top of any frozen pie and place in the freezer to set.

Another option is to warm the cream by letting the blender run for 3 minutes. Serve it as a sauce over baked figs, poached pears, or Abuela's Glazed Bananas (page 262).

BEYOND THE KALE

Find Your Purpose & Invest in the Journey

On the surface, this lifestyle is all about eating amazing food and feeling great. Taking out an insurance policy against disease. Investing in ourselves, our children, and the planet at large.

But there is so much more at play. Because food is the portal to the soul. A powerful starting point to catalyze an entirely new perspective on the self, the world around us, and our place in it.

When I began this journey, my goals were simple: lose the belly fat; avoid a heart attack; and enjoy my children at their energy level. I achieved those goals, and then some. But what I didn't realize at the time was that this was just the beginning. Eight years later I can honestly say that this lifestyle changed everything about me. Who I am. What is important. And the person I have become. An unexpected but amazing journey toward wholeness. An exploratory quest to become my best, most authentic self.

The greatest gift of adopting
this way of eating and living
extends far beyond the plate.

For me it started with questions. Small questions relating to nutrition morphing into much bigger questions about life, and my place in the world. *Who am I really? What is truly important? What do I want to express and give in my short time here on Earth?*

I now look at the world through a new pair of glasses.

We live in a curious time when literally everything has become about facilitating comfort and ease. Our cultural mandate has become the elimination of obstacles and challenges, the brass ring achievement defined by leisure— a life free of stress, pain, hardship, and struggle. Meanwhile, our focus is keenly placed on the accumulation of *stuff,* most of which is specifically designed to make our lives easier, more comfortable. We are brainwashed into believing

that flat-screen TVs, high-speed Internet, new shoes, a fancy car, and designer pharmaceuticals for every conceivable ailment, imagined or otherwise, hold the key to our identity, and ultimately our happiness.

The United States is the most prosperous nation in the world, and yet our *citizenship* has been comprehensively reduced to *consumerism*. A culture in which our primary directive is the quest to accumulate this *stuff*, or at least more than our friends and neighbors. *Buy and ye shall be happy.*

But what have we truly purchased? In the words of my favorite poet, Henry David Thoreau, *"The mass of men lead lives of quiet desperation,"* our lives prostrate at the altar of the false gods of our instant-gratification society. A culture of emasculated drones more depressed, obese, diseased, stressed, lethargic, medicated, generally unhappy, and overall unfulfilled than any other culture on the planet. An entrenched, self-perpetuating cycle then ensues that drives us to further escape, salving our pain and disillusionment with unhealthy food choices, television, video games, alcohol, illicit drugs and pharmaceuticals, shopping, gambling, or unhealthy relationships; you name it. The hole never gets filled, of course—it just grows deeper. An endless pit of woe to which we willingly enslave ourselves. A succumbing, in the ethos of Thoreau, to the *delusion of need*. A profound lunacy that is bankrupting our souls and decimating our planet.

Most of all, we're *sick*. Sicker than we've ever been, on both an individual and a planetary level. And if we continue along this path, the prognosis is bleak. In truth, we're in the midst of an almost unspeakable, unsustainable health care and environmental crisis. Despite spending over $22 billion a year on fad diet and weight-loss products, 70 percent of all Americans are obese or overweight. Childhood obesity rates are through the roof. One out of every three deaths in America is attributable to heart disease, our number one killer. And by 2030, studies predict that close to 50 percent of Americans will be diabetic or prediabetic. In response, we have become indentured servants to the pharmaceutical industry, popping pills that effectively mask symptoms but more often than not do little or nothing to prevent or cure our underlying chronic ailments. Meanwhile, our factory-farm system is irrevocably depleting our soil. And livestock harvesting is polluting our bodies with saturated fat, hormones, pesticides, and GMOs, all while decimating the environment at an unfathomable rate.

Our reaction? Grab a beer, pop a pill, order a pizza, and leave me alone because *Honey Boo Boo* is on the TiVo. No wonder we're so unhealthy, unhappy, depressed, and desperate.

True happiness is an inside job. It is unlocked only when we crack the hardened crust of our protective social armor to delve deeply and honestly into what drives us. It is forged through struggles, challenges, and failures to elucidate personal growth, self-knowledge, and ultimately fulfillment through selfless service to others, as well as to the authentic self within. This is hardly a new concept, and yet happiness eludes most people. Intellectually we understand this to be the case and yet most of us simply shirk away, slinking back into our chimerical zone of comfort and denial like an addict to the opium den. A world of conforming to societal expectations, doing what we're told. Buying stuff and keeping quiet. Indeed, *The Matrix*.

I know this because I've been there. Just eight years ago, I was a classic couch potato: fifty pounds overweight, overworked, lethargic, depressed, and subsisting almost entirely on what I like to call the *window diet*—if it could be handed to me through my car window at the drive-through, I ate it. A black belt at "checking out," for decades the solution to my emotional pain was to self-medicate with drugs, alcohol, fast food, and unhealthy relationships—a path that took me to some very dark and desperate places.

I was also in the midst of what you might call an existential crisis. Despite advanced degrees from prestigious universities and a promising career track, I was a walking risk-averse calculation, devoid of passion yet compelled forward by the mythic, undeniable allure of the American Dream—only to discover it a false, transparent veneer. Eventually the pain became so great, the only solution was to let it all go or die. Pain works that way. It sucks. But it's also the greatest imaginable catalyst for change. So if you're feeling it, consider yourself lucky.

The good news is that there is a solution. A solution that begins and ends with what you put in your mouth. *And then becomes something else entirely:* a spiritual journey toward wholeness.

My personal version of this odyssey began with a decision to adopt a plant-based diet at the age of forty, followed by a search for answers in the crucible of physical suffering—countless hours spent pedaling a bike, running ridiculous distances, and staring at a black line at the bottom of a pool as I trained for the ludicrous endurance-fest known as the Ultraman World Championships. It wasn't just illogical, it was utterly baffling in its relationship to rationality. And yet deep within the recesses of my soul, I knew with every aspect of my being that it was what I was meant to be doing. *It's what made my heart beat hardest.*

Julie—bless her soul—had the capacity to see this truth. Rather than dissuade me with arrows of reason, she pushed me to continue when faith faltered and the mind strove to reclaim the reins. Why? Because she knew my drive emanated from something pure. True. And unmistakably dire. Despite all that is rational, my life depended upon this particular brand of physically and mentally excruciating soul exploration as a means to resolve the seemingly unresolvable personal crisis I then endured.

Somehow I found the means to temporarily quell the endless deterring chatter of the thinking mind. To be fair, fear retained a strong foothold of precious real estate in my consciousness. It still does. But I found the wherewithal to nonetheless propel forward in the face of it. And ignore the often unbearable social pressures relentlessly driving to derail me. I focused on the heart. I relied on faith. I got comfortable with the uncomfortable. I embraced the mystery of not knowing what the next day might bring. And at every turn, I concentrated on how I could be of service to others. Because there is gigantic, undeniable truth in the edict that when you give, you get back tenfold.

As a result, I have somehow persevered. Emerged into a new life. It is, in fact, an impossible, astounding life beyond what I could have previously imagined, let alone thought possible. A direct result of nothing other than a decision—followed by relentless daily action toiling in obscurity—to embrace something we are all too often socially compelled to repress and ignore: *the heart that beats hardest.*

Plant-based nutrition didn't just repair my health. It was the key that unlocked my heart. It was the catalyst that made my entire crazy journey possible by unleashing an internal personal power I never thought possible to actualize the best, most authentic version of myself.

It wasn't quick. It wasn't easy. Nor linear or pretty. It took deep reserves of previously untapped resolve. It required confronting powerful dissuasion both external and internal. It is *the warrior path.* And yet I wouldn't trade it for anything; it is worth every failure, bead of sweat, and sleepless night I've endured.

Not everyone wants to be an ultra-endurance athlete. I get that. The point is that we all have a better, healthier, more authentic version of ourselves locked within, yearning to be expressed. If I could change so drastically, I know for a fact this powerful reality resides within all of us. My hope is that my example inspires you to understand that change is possible. But inspiration is just a first step—a fleeting spark that, left to its own devices, quickly flickers and fades, often failing to yield any tangible positive outcome.

But why? There are many reasons. We underestimate the profound grip of addiction to foods and behavior patterns that don't serve us. The emotional pathways that keep us stuck. The looping of a thinking mind that resists change.

above all. Our collective discomfort with the unknown. Poor self-esteem and lifelong feelings of inadequacy and unworthiness. The inability to properly plan and execute a goal. But more than anything, we fail because we are *afraid.*

We've all been there. It's why most can't sustain a diet. It's the reason we are hopelessly incapable of keeping lost weight off for good; abandon New Year's resolutions shortly after their announcement; remain stuck in jobs we don't like; and mute our persistent emotional pain with distractions like television, video games, and shopping.

I'm interested in the mystery that lies beyond the first step. I'm interested in focusing on the *long walk* that follows.

Our goal—and the goal of this book—is to provide you with the tools necessary to bridge that elusive gap between inspiration and implementation. Tools that will catalyze and sustain the *action-based change* you seek but to date have failed to achieve. Tools that will help you unlock and unleash your best, most authentic self. A fully actualized "you" in mind, body, and spirit that extends far beyond the delicious meal gracing your plate.

We begin by making a choice to invest not in results, but in the journey ahead. First, we feed ourselves with high-vibrating food. Then, we look inward. Because you simply cannot become the person you are meant (and deserve) to be without self-awareness, self-knowledge, and a deep connection with what moves you. It's truly an inside job that requires patience. But most of all, *faith.*

It's not easy. In fact, it just might be the hardest thing imaginable. Fear, logic, ego, friends, and family dissuade. Every aspect of the thinking mind is in revolt. Because pursuing life premised on faith and passion isn't about thinking—it's what thinking was designed to prevent. It's not logical in any way, shape, or form. It threatens every dark corner of identity, status quo, and our hardwired drive for social acceptance and approval. A terrifying reveal of "identity" as pure fiction—mere stories we tell ourselves about who we are and why we do what we do to comfort us against the paralyzing unknowable—that forces us and others to confront the truth about choices made.

A truly objective look in the mirror usually isn't pleasant. Armed in denial, we go to great lengths to avoid this act. I know I do. It takes tremendous courage to quiet external noise. Even more courage to quell the internal rebellion—the voice of the mind that destroys imagination, levels wonder, and clutches to fear and illusion with an impossible death grip.

Faith stands in denial of reason. In order to pursue a life of passion, the mind must be destroyed. Comfort in unknowingness. An embrace of the void.

I am not suggesting you ignore real-world responsibilities. Only that it is my direct personal experience that the limits we impose upon ourselves are generally illusory. And driven predominantly by fear. Fear of failure. Fear of success. Fear of the unknown. Fear of discomfort. Fear of financial insecurity. Fear of what others might think. All told, fear of everything. And fear is not your friend. Not now, not ever.

To echo Thoreau, *we need not lead lives of quiet desperation.* You can break the chains of enslavement to take control of your health, your fitness, your profession, your relationships, and yes, your destiny. And no matter what your circumstances, it's never too late.

I do not promise that a heart-based life will result in financial reward, fancy friends, notoriety, or even a single Facebook "like." But I do make one promise: that such an exploration will infuse your life with a meaning and sense of purpose you cannot now predict. Happiness—not in a blissed-out, unicorns-and-rainbows sense, but rather a deep satisfaction that your life has value. A value that is infectious and can be shared. Passed on as inspiration in service to others who feel impossibly stuck. Imprisoned by a life not of their conscious choosing but often compelled by circumstance; and the perils of the thinking mind—an organ wired to prioritize comfort, security, and avoidance of fear and challenge over adventure and the depth of experience.

This is your call to action. Set aside your preconceived notions. Let go of habits that don't serve you. Challenge your self and your assumptions. Invest in adventure. Do whatever it takes to find and unlock that thing that makes your heart beat hardest. Then take the leap. And embrace the struggle that follows. In fact, welcome it with every fiber of your being. Throw yourself into the muck, put yourself on the line, and stare it right in the face.

But most of all? Dream big. Whatever the result, seize the opportunity to learn something about yourself. Apply it. *Grow.* Then watch as a better, more authentic self begins to surface. I'm here to say it's worth the journey. And at the end of the day, there is nothing but the journey. Because destination is pure illusion.

This is what it means to go beyond the kale. This is the warrior path. This is the art of living with purpose.

SAUCES + DRESSINGS

J THE SECRET IS THE SAUCE

Many of our "secret" sauces were key in helping us to go completely plant-based. No matter how you are feeling, the time of day, season, recipe, dish, or meal, our sauces will not fail you. I have had large chain-restaurant owners hunt me down for certain recipes.

Getting familiar with preparing these sauces is a vital step in creating weekly meals for you and your family. The good news? They all take less than fifteen minutes to prepare!

I hope you enjoy them and use them creatively.

CANDIED GINGER ISLAND CRANBERRY SAUCE

My family loves cranberry sauce! And not just around the holidays, but really for any rainy day when thoughts turn to nurturing comfort food. This recipe was created while we were living in yurts on an organic farm in Kauai a couple of years back. We had some friends over from Los Angeles to enjoy Thanksgiving dinner in the yurt kitchen lab; we dined to the symphony of tropical rain showers pelting our canvas roof in sheets. Our vegan meal was especially delightful, even to the meat eaters in our group. The aromatic ginger combined with cranberries makes this an exotic, lively twist on the traditional cranberry sauce. My family demands it alongside Mashed Potatoes (page 224) and Tempeh Loaf (page 233).

Ingredients

• 2 (12-ounce) packages fresh cranberries

• ¼ cup filtered water

• 8 dates, soaked in filtered water for 30 minutes and pitted

• 1 cup candied ginger cubes

• Dash cinnamon

Preparation

1. In a small saucepan, simmer all the ingredients over medium heat until the cranberries and dates break down to form a sauce.

2. Adjust the sweetness to taste.

3. Cool and serve.

TAHINI GREEN SAUCE

A lighter version of its momma: hummus. This lemony sauce is pure bliss on your plate. The nutritional yeast provides a nice boost of B vitamins and a substantial amount of folic acid along with a cheesy taste. We serve it as a sauce over various One Bowls (page 197). Pour it over steamed kale, black beans, and quinoa. Add a baked yam with cinnamon sprinkled on it and you have a meal that is the foundation of wellness.

Ingredients

- 6 tablespoons raw organic tahini paste
- 2 tablespoons nutritional yeast
- Juice of 1 small lemon
- 1 teaspoon garlic powder
- ½ teaspoon Celtic sea salt, to taste
- ¼ cup fresh dill or cilantro
- 1 teaspoon maple syrup
- 1 tablespoon apple cider vinegar
- 1 cup filtered water

Preparation

1. To a Vitamix, high-powered blender, or food processor, add all the ingredients and blend.

2. If you keep the Vitamix going for a couple of minutes, it will automatically heat your sauce. Or you can transfer it to a saucepan and warm it up old school. Sometimes I prefer to do soups or sauces this way so I can easily adjust the seasoning. I also like to stir the sauce and infuse it with my love and healing intentions.

HUMMUS ODE TO MAXIME

Rich devoured hummus when he traveled to Beirut to spread the Plantpowered message to the "Paris" of the Middle East. This tasty dish transports Rich back to Lebanon, where he ran the beautiful coastline and cycled the cypress tree–peppered hills with Lebanon's most celebrated extreme athlete, Maxime Chaya. Hummus is truly one of the staples of eating tasty vegan food. This creamy, versatile spread can be flavored a number of different ways. In this recipe, I honor the authentic origin of the dish and add a fresh California twist with some herbs and seasonings. Hummus is the perfect addition to sandwiches, or you can serve it with raw veggies as a dip.

Ingredients

- 2 cups garbanzo beans
- 2 tablespoons raw organic tahini paste
- Juice of 1 large lemon
- 1 garlic clove
- 1 teaspoon sea salt
- Dash namah shoyu
- 1 tablespoon nutritional yeast
- 8 basil leaves, plus more for garnish
- 2½ tablespoons olive oil
- ¼ cup filtered water
- Dash paprika

Preparation

1. To a food processor or Vitamix, add the garbanzo beans, tahini, lemon juice, garlic, and sea salt. Blend until smooth.

2. Add the namah shoyu, nutritional yeast, and basil. Blend again on high.

3. With the motor running, remove the plastic cap of the lid and add the olive oil. Add small amounts of the filtered water until you achieve the desired consistency.

4. Turn the hummus out into a serving bowl and garnish with basil and paprika.

Chef's Note: You can use canned, dried, or sprouted garbanzo beans.

If you use dried garbanzo beans, soak them overnight and then boil on high until they are tender. Drain and cool.

If you use canned, drain and rinse the beans before adding them.

If you choose to sprout them, allow 5 days as they take a bit longer than smaller beans. I also boil them until tender rather than leaving them raw. It gives a smoother texture to the hummus.

SIMPLE MUSHROOM GRAVY

Upgrade your gravy to soothe and nourish body, mind, and soul! This healthy modern take on a classic holds its own. Packed with vitamins, minerals, and powerful antioxidants, this delicious recipe is a huge nutritional improvement upon traditional versions that rely on copious amounts of lard and refined flour.

Keep in mind, making the perfect gravy requires fine-tuning the salt and water contents every time to arrive at the ideal consistency and taste. Use a wide variety with a fair amount of darker-colored mushrooms for the best taste and color. Shiitake, shelf, and porcini are some of my favorite fungi varieties. However, skip the portabella—it will make the gravy taste too strong. Pour this silky delight over our Aromatic Country-Style Tempeh Loaf (page 233) or Mashed Potatoes (page 224) and enjoy the exotic healing powers of this woodland creation.

Ingredients

- 4 cups farmers' market mushrooms
- 1 tablespoon macadamia nut oil
- ½ small shallot
- ½ small lemon
- 2 tablespoons gluten-free tamari
- 1 to 1½ cups filtered water
- 1 teaspoon fresh rosemary
- 1 teaspoon fresh sage
- About 8 pitted Kalamata olives
- 2 tablespoons white sesame seeds, or ¼ cup raw cashews (optional)
- ½ teaspoon salt (optional)

Preparation

1. Wash and stem the mushrooms.

2. Heat the macadamia nut oil in a large skillet over medium heat and sauté the shallot until brown. Add the mushrooms and sauté them for about 5 minutes, until they begin to brown and release their juices.

3. Turn the heat off and squeeze the lemon over the mushrooms. Add the tamari and stir.

4. Transfer the mushrooms to a Vitamix or high-powered blender and puree until smooth. Add ½ cup of the water, the rosemary, sage, and half the olives. Process again until smooth. Taste for seasoning and add the remaining olives, if desired.

5. If you like a creamier gravy, or one lighter in color, add the sesame seeds or cashews. Process in the Vitamix until well blended.

6. Pour the mushroom puree back into the skillet and add the remaining filtered water, ½ cup at a time, until the gravy reaches the desired consistency. If it needs more salt, add another splash of tamari or ½ teaspoon sea salt.

SECRET TOMATO SAUCE

One of my signature sauces, this is a buttery, full-flavored tomato sauce. The cacao nibs really deepen the flavor while adding a healthy dose of essential nutrients, vitamins A, C, E, lycopene, and antioxidants. Lycopene helps to protect you against many types of cancer. And the pine and Brazil nuts make the sauce a velvety smooth delight. It works wonderfully in our Portabella Parmesana (page 205) or served over gluten-free penne. Try it and you'll immediately know why this sauce is one of our favorites.

Ingredients

- 1 cup organic cherry tomatoes
- 3 dehydrated sun-dried tomatoes
- 2 Brazil nuts
- 2 tablespoons pine nuts
- 1 tablespoon cacao nibs
- 2 tablespoons olive oil
- Celtic sea salt, to taste

Preparation

1. In a wok or cast-iron skillet using no oil, slightly blacken the cherry tomatoes on high heat. If the pan is hot, this should take no more than 5 minutes.

2. To a blender or Vitamix, add the cherry tomatoes and all the other ingredients. Blend on high for a full minute. Adjust the seasoning to taste.

WALNUT PÂTÉ

This recipe came into my life during a time when I was experimenting with nuts. My mind was filled with lucid dreams of vibrant and purifying green cilantro leaves clearing heavy metals from my blood cells. The world started spinning and I heard, "They are the eggman, I am the walnut!" You know the rest. Truly, this spread will become an obsession for your taste buds—the flavors are nothing short of intoxicating. Walnuts are brain food rich with antioxidants and cilantro is a wonderful detoxifier. Serve this pâté on warm bread, a flax cracker, or a collard green and you'll know what all the fuss is about. . . . Enjoy!

Ingredients

- 1 large bunch fresh cilantro
- 1½ cups raw walnuts
- 1 (6.5-ounce) jar pitted Kalamata olives, drained
- Filtered water

Preparation

1. To a Vitamix or food processor, add the entire bunch of cilantro, followed by the nuts and the olives. Blend on medium speed, using the plunger attachment to carefully distribute the ingredients so they can be processed evenly. It may take a couple of times of rearranging the cilantro so that it gets completely broken down. Add small amounts of filtered water to achieve a spreadable consistency.

2. Transfer to a small serving dish and serve!

FAST RAW MOLE

This is a very rich, cacao-perfumed sauce with tons of flavor. The traditional recipe takes four days to make. My version takes less than thirty minutes and comes to the table with a healthy kick. Loaded with antioxidants, anti-inflammatory properties, fiber, vitamins, and healthy omega-3 fats, it's a tantalizing sauce that excites! Serve this with our Tamales de Regalos (page 210) or Aztec Enchiladas (page 214).

Ingredients

- 3 dates, pitted
- ½ cup blanched raw almonds
- ½ cup dried ancho chili powder, or 3 whole dried ancho chilies
- Filtered water
- 1 pound cherry tomatoes
- 5 tomatillos
- 1 tablespoon chili powder
- 8 cherries, pitted, or farm-fresh blackberries
- ¼ cup cacao powder
- 1 handful cacao nibs
- 2 tablespoons maple syrup
- Celtic sea salt, to taste (about 1 teaspoon)

Preparation

1. Soak the dates, almonds, and ancho chilies, if using, separately in small bowls filled with hot filtered water. Set aside for at least 30 minutes.

2. In a wok or cast-iron skillet, using no oil, slightly blacken the cherry tomatoes over high heat. This should take no more than 3 minutes. You want to see only a touch of black on one side of the tomatoes. The juices will start to release, but the tomatoes should still be firm and fresh.

3. Transfer the tomatoes straight into a Vitamix or high-powered blender.

4. Remove the skins from the tomatillos and slightly blacken them using the same technique as above.

5. Slice the soaked ancho chilies, if using, lengthwise, scrape out the seeds, and remove the stems. (Reserve ¼ cup of the soaking water.)

6. Add the chilies or ancho chili powder, soaked almonds, and soaked pitted dates to the tomatoes in the Vitamix or high-powered blender. Blend until the mixture is smooth.

7. Now add all the remaining ingredients and reserved soaking water and blend again. Adjust the seasonings to taste.

Chef's Note: For a healthier version, try leaving out the oil altogether. If you want more kick, add some jalapeño or cayenne pepper! This sauce can be kept for 3 days in the refrigerator.

BLACKENED TOMATO CASHEW SAUCE

A rich, hearty, homestyle tomato sauce that really creates a comforting meal in minutes. Serving a healthy dose of lycopene from the tomatoes and omega-3 fats from the cashews, this simple sauce is delightful. It's almost completely raw and takes all of three minutes to prepare. It's great over pasta or as a soup. But we use it as a delicious sauce over our Aromatic Country-Style Tempeh Loaf (page 233), and it smothers our Vegan Lasagna (page 236) as well. Learn to make it by heart. It will leave you wondering why you ever bought that jar of tomato sauce.

Ingredients

- 1 pound cherry tomatoes
- ¼ red bell pepper
- ¼ cup raw cashews
- 3 dehydrated sun-dried tomatoes
- 2 tablespoons olive oil
- 1 tablespoon vegan butter spread (i.e., Earth Balance)
- 1 small carrot
- Celtic sea salt, to taste

Preparation

1. In a cast-iron skillet or wok, blacken the tomatoes whole over high heat with no oil.

2. Remove the seeds and stem of the bell pepper. Blacken in the same pan using no oil.

3. Transfer the slightly blackened tomatoes and bell pepper to a Vitamix or high-powered blender and add all the remaining ingredients except the sea salt. The sun-dried tomatoes will add a fair amount of salt, so blend first and then add sea salt to taste.

Chef's Note: If you don't have cashews, you can use Brazil or macadamia nuts.

If you are on the Transformation path, skip the vegan butter, cashews, and olive oil.

ALMOND PESTO

4–6

This sweet basil and almond mix celebrates a healthier you. A truly inspired twist on the standard Italian pesto recipe—known for its pine nuts and Parmesan cheese—this is the perfect plant-based version: a beautiful sauce that is downright delectable, one of our top-five recipes ever. It's almost impossible to believe that there is no cheese in this full-bodied cheesy-tasting pesto, which is the secret ingredient in our delectable Vegan Lasagna (page 236), Portabella Parmesana (page 205), and Gluten-Free Spaghetti di Pesto (page 220). Pour it over gluten-free pasta or use it as a sandwich spread to take your panini to a whole new level. In a word, *bello!*

Ingredients

- Leaves from 2 large bunches basil (about 2 cups)
- 1 cup raw almonds
- 1 tablespoon olive oil
- Juice of 1 medium lemon
- 1 teaspoon large-grain Celtic sea salt
- Filtered water

Preparation

1. To a Vitamix, high-powered blender, or food processor, add the basil leaves, almonds, olive oil, lemon juice, and salt. You may have to stop and scrape down the sides of the container so that the basil gets completely blended into a paste.

2. Add very small amounts of filtered water, 1 tablespoon at a time, to achieve the desired consistency. For a spread, use less water; for a sauce, use a bit more.

BRAZIL NUT TOMATILLO CREAM

We are so happy that our Tomatillo Salsa (page 104) and Brazil Nut Cream Spread (page 79) found each other! Blossoming with fresh cilantro, green tomatillos, lime juice, and garlic, these delectable tastes make for a lively sauce. Packed with essential vitamins, minerals, and antioxidants, this cream will heal your body and soul. A beautiful union of flavors that makes a delightful addition to any Mexican food meal, this recipe also serves as a delicious sandwich spread or a dip for chips or veggies. Enjoy it with our Cauliflower Golden Beet Tacos (page 222).

Ingredients

- 8 tomatillos
- 2 garlic cloves
- 1 bunch cilantro
- Juice of 1 small lime
- 8 Brazil nuts
- 1 small jalapeño
- ½ teaspoon Celtic sea salt

Preparation

1. Remove the skins from the tomatillos and cut them in half.

2. In a cast-iron skillet or wok, blacken the tomatillos over high heat on one side only. Transfer to a Vitamix or food processor.

3. Mash the garlic with the side of a large knife. Remove and discard the green center sprout.

4. Add the mashed garlic, cilantro bunch with stems, some lime juice, the Brazil nuts, and the jalapeño to the blender. Blend on high. Add the sea salt and another squeeze of lime. Blend again and adjust the seasonings to taste.

2 SALSAS

The best of amigos, these salsas are a harmonious pairing of flavors at the end of your tortilla chip. The Tomatillo version is a great mild salsa that has the cleansing properties of cilantro and lime. Our Ginger version features juicy heirloom tomatoes that are glorious for your skin, with a nice kick of ginger to aid digestion.

Using a food processor, salsa prep time is under ten minutes. So don't wait for a special occasion to create a healthy salsa for your family. Tonight's the night! Say "good-bye" to the processed store-bought varieties and "hello" to your new best friend.

Tomatillo Salsa

A beautiful blend of fresh ingredients come together to make this classic green salsa. This is a mild salsa that adds flavor rather than heat. We use this in our Tamales de Regalos (page 210), Torre de Nachos (page 207) and Tempeh Chili (page 165). Skip the jalapeño entirely if you have little ones.

Ingredients

- 8 tomatillos
- ¼ cup olive oil
- ½ cup fresh cilantro
- Juice of 1 small lime
- ½" piece jalapeño, seeded
- 1 teaspoon Celtic sea salt

Preparation

1. Remove the skins from the tomatillos and cut them in half.

2. In a cast-iron skillet or wok over very high heat, slightly blacken the tomatillos on one side using no oil.

3. Transfer directly to a food processor.

4. Add the olive oil, cilantro, lime juice, jalapeño, and sea salt. Pulse intermittently until the mixture is the desired consistency. Go slowly, as it will take only 7 pulses or so. If you overpulse, the salsa will become liquid. Adjust the salt to taste.

Ginger Heirloom Salsa

Raw ginger gives this pico de gallo a pop of flavor and aids digestion. Combined with antioxidant-rich tomatoes, it's a happy, healthy combination. Try this with chips or add it to your next meal.

Ingredients

- 1 red heirloom tomato
- 1 green heirloom tomato
- 2 tablespoons olive oil
- ½" piece fresh ginger, peeled
- ½" piece jalapeño, seeded

Preparation

To a food processor, Vitamix, or high-powered blender, add all the ingredients and pulse sparingly, only 6 to 8 times. This will yield a thick, chunky salsa.

LEMON GUACAMOLE

Beautiful. Simple. Alive. This recipe may have only three ingredients, but it's the perfect taste trifecta. Filled with skin-smoothing vitamins A, C, E, and K, avocados boast one of the highest amino-acid contents of all fruit and also have healthy fats to lubricate the digestive tract. The combination of lemon juice with avocado is a heavenly match. But you won't think of that while you're eating it because it just tastes so GOOD! This recipe is hands down Rich's favorite, finding its way into his regimen almost daily.

Ingredients

- 4 ripe avocados
- Juice of 1 large lemon, plus more to taste
- 2 teaspoons Celtic sea salt

Preparation

1. Cut the avocados in half, remove the pits, saving the largest one, and scoop the flesh out of the skins right into a shallow bowl.

2. Using a knife, cut the avocado flesh to make cubes.

3. Add the juice of an entire lemon over the avocados and continue cutting until you have small-diced pieces.

4. Add the sea salt and more lemon juice to taste.

5. Place the reserved pit in the center of the guacamole. This will keep it from turning brown. Store it in the fridge, covered.

Chef's Note: For an Ayurvedic version, substitute 3 limes for the lemon juice and add fresh ground black pepper.

4-6

RAW PEANUT SAUCE

The creation of this sauce arose from a burning question I have been harboring for decades: "Just what on earth is inside that bottled jar of peanut sauce?" After some meditative contemplation, the creative inspiration for a homemade blend of fresh and lively sauciness came over me and a new kind of peanut sauce was born. The result is nothing short of amazing. Make sure you use virgin jungle peanuts. They are pinkish in color and give this sauce a vibrant, alive flavor that only this variety of raw peanut can deliver. If you don't have a specialty health market in your area, you can order these nuts online.

Ingredients

- ¾ cup virgin jungle peanuts
- 2 cups filtered water
- 1 date, soaked and pitted
- 1 tablespoon coconut oil
- 1 small garlic clove (optional)
- 1 teaspoon paprika
- Dash cayenne pepper
- ½ teaspoon Celtic sea salt

Preparation

1. Soak the peanuts in 1 cup of the filtered water overnight.

2. Drain the peanuts and transfer them to a Vitamix or high-powered blender.

3. Add the date, coconut oil, garlic (if using), paprika, cayenne pepper, sea salt, and remaining 1 cup filtered water. Process for a full minute.

4. Adjust the thickness by adding more water in increments of 2 tablespoons at a time.

5. Adjust the seasonings, adding garlic, salt, or another date as desired.

FERMENTED PROBIOTIC KRAUT

Here is our favorite whole-food recipe for fermented kraut. Probiotics help populate a healthy gut. It's not a head trip. It's all in your gut. Add it to your meals wherever possible to experience vibrant health.

Ingredients

- 1 head purple cabbage
- 2 heads Chinese cabbage
- 3 medium beets
- 4" piece fresh ginger
- 1 (1.4-ounce) package dulse seaweed
- Filtered water
- 3 tablespoons Celtic sea salt

Preparation

1. Finely slice the cabbage heads, discarding the tough core and stem pieces. We like our kraut on the finer side, so make sure you slice the sections very thin, approximately ⅛" thick. Wash the beets and the ginger, then grate them with the skins on. Soak the dulse in filtered water and pull it apart in thin sections.

2. In a large jar (we prefer a 1-gallon glass jar), start to add the ingredients in layers. Begin with the purple cabbage, then the Chinese cabbage, some beets, some ginger, and finally seaweed. Sprinkle salt between the vegetables. Repeat the layers, sprinkling sea salt generously in between them, until you have used up all your ingredients.

3. Add weight to the top of the mixture by filling a large mason jar with water and setting it in the opening of the large glass jar on top of the kraut mixture.

4. Water should start to appear to just cover your kraut. If it doesn't come up fully, add a bit of salted filtered water to reach the surface.

5. Remove the weight, cover the kraut with a kitchen cloth, and secure with a rubber band. Let it sit at room temperature inside a cabinet or in a dark spot for 2 to 3 weeks.

6. When the fermenting is complete, after approximately 2 to 3 weeks, skim off the top layer and discard. Transfer the kraut to mason jars, seal, and store in the refrigerator. Then get started on the next batch. Just add the veggies to the leftover brine and begin the process all over again. You can go completely classic and leave out the beet, or add jalapeño, turmeric, celery seed, herbs, or garlic. Experiment and have fun!

Chef's Note: Check the mixture every few days and remove any mold that has set up at the top. The mold has to do with the mixture being in contact with air. If the brine liquid is not covering it, you will get mold. Just lift it off and discard. The mixture below the brine is fine. The kraut will smell and taste like sauerkraut, lively and a bit vinegar-like. If you smell anything foul or putrid, you didn't use enough salt, or you added too much water. Throw it out and chalk it up to experience!

CAESAR SALAD DRESSING

A zesty grown-up edition of Caesar dressing, this recipe's nice burst of garlic, lemony flavor, and creamy blended cashews come together to give your taste buds a treat. Filled with B vitamins, omega-3 fats, and detoxifying garlic and lemon juice, this healthy seasoned dressing on your salad will let you feel your best.

Ingredients

- ½ cup raw cashews
- 2 tablespoons nutritional yeast
- ½ teaspoon Celtic sea salt
- 1 small garlic clove
- 2 tablespoons avocado
- 1 teaspoon Dijon mustard
- 1 teaspoon vegan Worcestershire sauce
- 1 teaspoon dried seaweed flakes
- Juice of 1 large lemon
- ⅛ teaspoon cracked black pepper
- ½ cup filtered water
- Crumbled Walnut Parmesan (page 78)

Preparation

1. In a food processor, pulse the nuts until mealy in texture. Add the nutritional yeast, salt, and garlic and pulse again.

2. Add the avocado, Dijon, Worcestershire, seaweed flakes, lemon juice, cracked pepper, and water. Process for 30 seconds. Adjust the seasonings to taste.

3. Sprinkle with Crumbled Walnut Parmesan.

Chef's Note: For a child-friendly Caesar Salad Dressing, use 2 tablespoons Vegenaise, a splash of olive oil, juice of 1 small lemon, and Celtic sea salt to taste.

CLASSIC DIJON HONEY DRESSING

A gourmet dressing for when I long for the flavors of the French countryside, this golden blend adds life to any raw or warm salad but also works well with roasted or grilled veggies, potatoes, asparagus, and artichokes. Apple cider vinegar is always my first choice of vinegars because it has a highly alkalizing effect on the body and wonderfully aids digestion. Go ahead and prepare a triple batch today and keep it in the fridge. Before long, you'll find yourself drizzling it on everything.

Ingredients

- 2 tablespoons high-quality Dijon mustard
- 1 teaspoon honey
- 2 tablespoons apple cider vinegar
- Juice of 1 small lemon
- 2 tablespoons filtered water
- Celtic sea salt
- ⅛ teaspoon cracked black pepper
- ¼ teaspoon fresh thyme
- ¼ teaspoon fresh dill
- 1 lavender bloom, from your garden or local farmers' market

Preparation

1. Add all the ingredients to a mason jar, screw on the lid, and shake. Adjust the seasonings to taste. This dressing will keep up to a week in the refrigerator. If you like, triple the quantity and make a full jar.

Chef's Note: This is a no-oil dressing. But if you like, you can add 2 tablespoons olive oil or 4 olives pureed in ¼ cup water in the Vitamix or blender.

CREAMY AVOCADO DRESSINGS

Avocados make a wonderful, smooth base for a heavier dressing. Experiment with different herbs and spices. You can't go wrong. Feel free to omit the oil, if desired. Avocados are known for their combination of good fat and fiber, which helps control blood sugar levels. Mixed with fresh-squeezed lemon juice and a pinch of salt, this rich, creamy dressing always has people asking, "Yum, what's in this?"

Here are our two family favorites.

Farm
Ingredients

- ¼ small avocado
- Juice of 1 lemon
- ½ teaspoon Celtic sea salt
- 2 tablespoons grape seed oil
- 1 tablespoon fresh dill
- 2 tablespoons filtered water
- ⅛ teaspoon cracked black pepper

Preparation

1. Blend all the ingredients in a Vitamix or high-powered blender until smooth.

2. Adjust the seasoning to taste.

Spicy
Ingredients

- ¼ small avocado
- Juice of 1 lime
- Celtic sea salt
- 2 tablespoons olive oil
- ⅛" piece jalapeño
- 1 tablespoon fresh cilantro
- 2 tablespoons filtered water
- ⅛ teaspoon cracked black pepper

Preparation

1. Blend all the ingredients in a Vitamix or high-powered blender until smooth.

2. Adjust the seasoning to taste.

GRAPEFRUIT MISO DRESSING

4-6

Asian inspired and perfect for any summer salad, this grapefruit miso is light, flavorful, and easy to prepare. Make sure the grapefruits you select are sweet and in season. Combining fresh ginger, grapefruit juice, a touch of coconut oil, and miso provides a whole host of health benefits. Let the bounty of vitamins, minerals, antioxidants, and probiotics work together to support healthy digestion. Lovely to serve over shredded cabbage or kale.

Ingredients

- 2 tablespoons miso paste
- 2 tablespoons filtered water
- Juice of 1 sweet grapefruit
- 1 tablespoon liquid coconut oil
- ½ teaspoon grated fresh ginger
- Pinch sea salt

Preparation

1. In a small bowl, or at the bottom of a large salad bowl, whisk together all the ingredients until combined.

2. Adjust the seasoning to taste.

Chef's Note: If your coconut oil is hardened, simply place the jar in hot water for a few minutes to liquefy it.

ASIAN DRESSING

This dressing has a wonderfully light, lemony blend of flavors that will make any salad shine. You can adjust the consistency by experimenting with the amounts of lemon juice and filtered water. The fermented miso is a great source of healthy probiotic bacteria to help your gut break down proteins and carbohydrates. Meanwhile, the lemon juice is a wonderful detoxifying citrus. This is a perfect tropical dressing for Hula Kale Salad (page 180) or Raw Asian Salad (page 183).

Ingredients

- ¼ cup chickpea miso (or yellow soy miso)
- 2 tablespoons liquid coconut oil or sesame oil
- Juice of 1 large lemon
- 2 tablespoons filtered water
- 1 tablespoon gluten-free tamari
- 1 tablespoon apple cider vinegar

Preparation

In the bottom of a large wooden bowl, whisk together the miso, coconut oil, lemon juice, filtered water, tamari, and vinegar.

Chef's Note: You can make the consistency of this dressing more liquid by adding more lemon juice. No salt is needed as the miso is already quite salty.

EVOLUTIONARY + REVOLUTIONARY

Our journey into whole vitality and wellness has been both evolutionary and revolutionary. It's an ever-changing process, one that is constantly evolving, shifting, and growing. Each of us must find our own unique path. There is no beginning or end. It's a process of creative discovery to understand all the layers of your true self and what supports your body, mind, and spirit in their highest expression. Eating lots of plants, meditation, yoga, fitness, music, art, and living creatively are what support our tribe. What supports yours?

BREAKFAST
+ BRUNCH

⏺ OUT OF THE BREAKFAST BOX

The recipes in the following sections work well for an everyday breakfast, a weekend brunch, or a late-night snack and will satisfy you when you are craving breakfast for dinner or something beyond the ordinary mealtime lineup.

Who made the rules about what constitutes appropriate breakfast fare? Hold on tight, because it's time to upend everything you thought you knew about the morning meal.

Our family generally kick-starts the day by "drinking a salad" in the form of a green smoothie or fresh-pressed vegetable juice, often complemented with a large bowl of oatmeal or protein-rich quinoa porridge. But the winning breakfast choice in our house is pudding. Chia Seed Pudding (page 138), to be exact—a superfood-infused delight packed with nutrition and giving a long-lasting energy boost. Eating pudding for breakfast sounds wonderfully rebellious, doesn't it?

Our kids think so, which is why this dish was instrumental in warming our children up to the idea of eating plant-based. Imagine our surprise some months later when strange new delicacies began to mysteriously appear on our kids' breakfast plates—crazy things like piping-hot miso soup, steamed green beans and broccoli, sautéed spinach, and baked yams sprinkled with cinnamon. One morning I was pleasantly shocked to see my ten-year-old, Mathis (always the vocal rebel), casually saunter by me carrying a huge plate of sautéed red chard retrieved from a pot of Red Chard Miso Soup (page 168) that was on the stove—at eight o'clock in the morning! It seemed so ludicrous, I burst out laughing.

The lesson? There are no rules, just choices. By preparing fun, "out of the box" healthy food options, you can boldly break the conventional breakfast game paradigm.

Family traditions, culture, and country of origin generally determine our morning meal proclivities. But these are habits, not laws. Toss out the playbook and rewrite the script to create a fun, new narrative limited only by the boundaries of your healthy imagination. Begin by introducing new breakfast tastes alongside familiar ones. Try offering steamed veggies and yams alongside that plate of pancakes. Try serving whole fruits from the farmers' market alongside the Tuscan Tofu Scramble (page 122). You get the picture. Based on my experience, it won't be long before both you and your children begin to happily opt for that steamed green bean, fresh artichoke, or bowl of berries before heading out to embrace the day.

TUSCAN TOFU SCRAMBLE

2–4

Scrambled tofu is my boys' favorite dish to whip up after returning home from a late-night gig. It has a neutral taste and egg-like texture, which you can flavor in many different ways. Consider it your blank canvas and get creative! Featuring juicy tomatoes with an accent of fragrant basil, this version has a little taste of the Italian countryside. But you don't have to stop here. Travel anywhere your heart desires—you can spice it up with the exotic pungent flavors of the Orient, or add the smoky, chipotle-rich flavors of Mexico—there are no limits! Sprouted, organic, and GMO-free tofu is always best.

Ingredients

- 1 tablespoon olive oil
- 1 garlic clove, crushed
- 1 (16-ounce) package organic sprouted tofu
- 1 cup Secret Tomato Sauce (page 98)
- 3 dashes gluten-free tamari
- 5 basil leaves, chopped, plus more for garnish
- 2 teaspoons Celtic sea salt
- 1 tablespoon nutritional yeast
- 2 tablespoons filtered water (optional)
- Fresh ground black pepper, to taste
- Cherry tomatoes, sliced, for garnish

Preparation

1. In a cast-iron skillet or saucepan, heat the olive oil over medium heat. Add the garlic and lightly sauté. Crumble the tofu right into the pan and mix well.

2. Add the tomato sauce, tamari, and basil. Stir to incorporate. Simmer for 3 minutes.

3. Sprinkle with sea salt and nutritional yeast; stir well. If the mixture gets too dry, add small amounts of filtered water. Cover and simmer to heat through.

4. Garnish with fresh cherry tomatoes, basil, and pepper.

HASH BROWNS TOWER

Juicy red beets, earthy mushrooms, and crispy hash brown potatoes pile on a medley of flavors packed with nutrients in this elegant tower of yum. Rich loves this one when he is in the mood for breakfast at dinnertime. I like it when I feel the need to impress.

Ingredients

- 1½ cups plus ¼ cup balsamic vinegar
- 2 tablespoons coconut sugar
- 2 medium beets
- 4 large portobello mushrooms
- 4 russet potatoes
- ¼ cup arrowroot powder
- ¼ cup ground flaxseeds
- 1 tablespoon finely chopped fresh rosemary
- 2 teaspoons Celtic sea salt, plus a pinch for the dressing
- ½ teaspoon fresh ground black pepper
- 2 tablespoons coconut oil
- 1 tablespoon olive oil
- Squeeze of fresh lemon juice
- 1 bunch fresh watercress
- ½ cup Brazil Nut Cream Spread (page 79)

recipe continues >>

Preparation

1. In a small saucepan, mix 1½ cups of the balsamic vinegar and the coconut sugar. Cook over medium-low heat, stirring the mixture continuously, until it reduces and thickens enough to coat the back of a spoon. This will be your balsamic glaze.

2. Preheat the oven to 350°F.

3. In a small saucepan, cook the beets in boiling water until tender, about 30 minutes. A fork should glide in easily.

4. While the beets are cooking, wash the mushrooms and remove the stems. Place them cap-side down, gills facing up, in a shallow baking dish with just enough water to cover the bottom of the pan without running over the mushrooms.

5. Pour 1 tablespoon of the remaining balsamic vinegar inside

each mushroom. Bake them for 15 minutes, or until tender. Remove from the oven and set aside.

6. Wash the potatoes well and grate them on a cheese or box grater into a large bowl.

7. Add the flaxseeds and arrowroot to the grated potato mixture. Then add the rosemary, sea salt, and pepper.

8. Pour the coconut oil into a large wok and heat over high heat. Tip the wok to coat it with the oil.

9. Using your hands, make a potato pancake out of the potato mixture and carefully place it in the wok. Using the same process, make three more pancakes. Brown the pancakes on one side to form a base and then turn and brown on the other side. Remove and set aside.

10. In a small bowl, combine the olive oil, lemon juice, and a pinch of sea salt. Mix well with a fork. Add the watercress and toss to coat.

11. Strain the water from the beets and remove the skins by rubbing them off with your fingers while running cold water over them. Cut into ⅛"-thick rounds.

12. Now it's time to build your hash brown towers. Start with a portobello mushroom, cap-side down. Spread some Brazil Nut Cream to fill the cap, then add a hash brown patty, a nice large beet slice, and finally top it all off with fresh watercress. Finish with a drizzle of the balsamic glaze, then stand back and smile!

MORNING PORRIDGE

No doubt about it, there is nothing quite like the nourishing quality of a great, traditional morning porridge. Enjoy this warming bowl at dawn to kick-start your metabolism, regulate your blood sugar, and provide you with a sustained, even-keeled energy to embrace the morning. Pure oatmeal is gluten-free. However, most brands are not pure, but are processed in the same facilities as grains like wheat, barley, or rye and so can contain small amounts of these. So if you're gluten-sensitive, make sure to read the label! Rich likes to mix quinoa into his porridge for an extra dose of morning protein. This version is inspired by the Indian healing practices of Ayurveda.

Ingredients

- 4 cups filtered water
- 1 cup oats
- 1 cup quinoa
- 4 teaspoons coconut oil
- 2 tablespoons cacao nibs
- 2 tablespoons dried goji berries
- ¼ cup raw walnuts
- ½ teaspoon cinnamon
- ½ teaspoon ground cardamom
- 1 teaspoon raw honey or maple syrup

Preparation

1. Bring the water to a boil and add the oats and quinoa. Reduce the heat to medium, cover, and simmer until the water is absorbed, the oatmeal is tender, and the quinoa is opened, about 20 minutes.

2. Ladle the porridge into beautiful individual serving bowls and make a small well in the center of each. For each bowl, spoon in 1 teaspoon of the coconut oil. Sprinkle ½ tablespoon of the cacao nibs around the outer edge, ½ tablespoon of the goji berries and 1 tablespoon walnuts in the center, and dust with cinnamon and cardamom. Finish by drizzling with raw honey or maple syrup.

Chef's Note: For a savory version, try using teff instead of quinoa, omit the sweetener, and add a generous pinch of sea salt. Garnish with fresh cilantro.

GLUTEN-FREE BERRY SCONES

Fresh baked scones that are healthy and gluten-free—can it be true? These scones are much lighter than a traditional full-butter scone and come with a side of those important omega-3 essential fats courtesy of the flaxseeds. You can experiment with different gluten-free flour options, combining two different flours in the same quantities as in this recipe. The flaxseed "eggs" and potato starch help hold them together. Remember: the trick with gluten-free baked goods is to let them cool a bit before removing them from the cookie sheet. They need to be transferred to a serving plate using a spatula and handled with care. Best served warm right out of the oven with raw honey and fresh jam.

Ingredients

- 2 tablespoons flaxseeds
- ¼ cup filtered water
- 1¼ cups brown rice flour
- ½ cup garbanzo flour
- 2 tablespoons potato starch
- 1 tablespoon baking powder
- 1 teaspoon xanthan gum
- 2 tablespoons date, coconut or, organic sugar
- ¼ cup coconut oil, chilled, plus more for greasing
- 2 cups Sweet Vanilla Almond Milk (page 75)
- 1 cup fresh blueberries
- 1 cup fresh raspberries
- 2 tablespoons powdered sugar
- Raw honey or jam, for serving

Preparation

1. Preheat the oven to 350°F.

2. In a small bowl, mix the flaxseeds and filtered water. Let stand for 2 minutes and then whisk until the mixture has an egg-like texture. If your mixture looks too dry, add a bit more filtered water. Set aside.

3. In a large bowl, sift together the brown rice flour, garbanzo flour, potato starch, baking powder, and xanthan gum.

4. Using a wooden spoon, add the date sugar and stir well.

5. Using a metal spoon, scoop out ¼" pieces of the hardened coconut oil and distribute evenly over the surface of the mixture. The secret to making scones is having the shortening—in our case, coconut oil—chilled and hard. This creates a flaky texture in the dough.

6. Using a knife, cut the coconut oil pieces into the dry mixture until well distributed.

7. When the mixture is mealy in texture and the coconut pieces are pea size, make a well in the center and add the almond milk and flaxseed "eggs." Mix everything together with a wooden spoon. Fold in the fresh berries. When the batter is ready, it should be sticky in texture.

8. On a coconut-oiled baking sheet, drop and arrange 3" sections of the scone mixture about 2" apart. They should be organic in shape, with a rough surface, like a drop cookie.

9. Bake for 18 to 20 minutes. Check the bottom by lifting one up with a spatula. You want the base established and brown but not burned. Keep your eye on them.

10. Let cool slightly, then and transfer to a serving plate. Sift powdered sugar over the top and drizzle with raw honey or serve with a dollop of jam.

ZUCCHINI BREAD

Everyone loves to eat zucchini when it's baked in moist, homemade bread. This loaf is full of flavor, yet remains light and airy in texture. We love this bread on a lazy Sunday morning or as a side to our hearty Tempeh Chili (page 165).

Ingredients

- ¼ cup coconut oil, plus more for greasing
- 6 tablespoons ground flaxseeds
- ½ cup warm filtered water
- 1 apple (red or pink local variety)
- 2 cups raw sugar
- 4 medium zucchini
- 2 cups sprouted spelt flour
- 1 cup sorghum flour
- ¾ teaspoon baking soda
- 1 tablespoon baking powder
- 1 tablespoon cinnamon
- 1 teaspoon Celtic sea salt

Preparation

1. Preheat the oven to 350°F.

2. Grease a large rectangular pan with coconut oil, making sure to coat the bottom and the sides well.

3. In a small bowl, whisk together the flaxseeds and ¼ cup of the warm water until they form an egg-like consistency.

4. Quarter the apple and remove the core and the seeds. Place in a Vitamix or high-powered blender with the remaining ¼ cup water and process until it makes a sauce.

5. In a medium bowl, combine the applesauce, flaxseed "eggs," coconut oil, and sugar; stir until combined.

6. Grate the zucchini into a shallow baking dish. Squeeze out the excess water and fold into the wet ingredients.

7. In a separate bowl, sift together the spelt flour, sorghum flour, baking soda, baking powder, cinnamon, and sea salt. Fold the dry mixture into the wet ingredients.

8. Pour into the prepared pan and even out the top with a rubber spatula.

9. Bake for 50 to 55 minutes, until a knife inserted into the center comes out clean. Let cool for a few minutes before slicing.

NO-LOX PLATE

This plate features many of the flavors of a traditional lox plate, except the star of this entrée is fresh veggies. A vibrant take on standard brunch fare, this dish will help you serve more vegetables during the breakfast hour. You might even find yourself upgrading that bagel to my preference, a thin slice of hemp bread or a buckwheat cracker. Get your morning nosh on and embrace this Plantpowered remake of a classic breakfast experience. Mazel tov!

Ingredients

- 3 large bunches spinach
- 1 teaspoon coconut oil
- 1 tablespoon namah shoyu or gluten-free tamari
- 2 large heirloom tomatoes
- 1 lemon
- 2 large avocados, pitted and peeled
- 4 sprouted wheat onion bagels, slices gluten-free bread, or buckwheat crackers
- 1 bunch fresh basil
- Handful sunflower seeds, sprouts, or local variety sprouts
- Himalayan salt or high-quality sea salt, to taste
- Fresh ground black pepper, to taste
- ½ cup whipped vegan cream cheese or Brazil Nut Cream Spread (page 79)

Preparation

1. Wash the spinach very well under cold water, making sure to remove any soil from the leaves. Spinach reduces down a great deal so I always triple whatever quantity I think I will need.

2. In a small saucepan, heat the coconut oil over high heat, add the spinach, and sauté until wilted. Remove from the heat and splash with the namah shoyu.

3. Slice the heirloom tomatoes, lemon, and avocados along with your choice of either bagels or bread.

4. Arrange all the vibrant ingredients, including the basil and sunflower seeds, beautifully on a large serving platter. Season with sea salt and pepper. Don't forget the cooked spinach. If you don't want to use packaged vegan cream cheese, opt for our Brazil Nut Cream Spread (page 79). Enjoy!

BLACKENED BOK CHOY

Believe it or not, our Plantpowered little girls love bok choy for breakfast! We love the preparation of this delicate green as it uses the beauty of the whole food in its entirety. This Chinese cabbage is an undeniably out-of-the-box breakfast choice. But once you get used to kicking off your day with this dish rich in vital phytonutrients, minerals, and health-benefiting antioxidants, you'll be coming back for more.

Ingredients

- 8 small heads bok choy
- 1 cup small brown mushrooms
- 1 teaspoon coconut oil
- ½ large lemon
- Celtic sea salt, to taste
- 2 tablespoons gluten-free tamari
- ¼ cup raw pepitas

Preparation

1. Slice any excess from the bok choy base stem without freeing all the leaves. Thoroughly rinse under water, gently opening the leaves to clear any soil from the base stems.

2. Remove the stems from the mushrooms; wash and cut the caps into thin slices.

3. In a dry wok or cast-iron skillet, blacken the bok choy over high heat using no oil. Turn and repeat on the other side. Arrange on a serving plate.

4. In the same cast-iron skillet or wok, heat the coconut oil. Add the mushrooms and sauté until they release their juices. Remove from the heat. Squeeze half the lemon over them and sprinkle with sea salt. Pour the mushroom mixture and tamari over the bok choy,

5. Garnish with the pepitas.

2–6

FARMERS' MARKET VEGGIES

Not sure what to do with all the beautiful veggies from the farmers' market? Open mouth. Insert veggie. Mindfully chew. Alternatively, pick up whatever speaks to you and try one of these easy methods. Be adventurous with more colors and flavors and real whole foods on your breakfast plate! PEACE + PLANTS

Steam

Steam only until the color brightens. Splash with gluten-free tamari and lemon juice.

Ingredients

- Lake green beans
- Broccoli
- Cauliflower
- Asparagus
- Artichoke

Sauté

Sauté in 1 teaspoon coconut oil. Splash with apple cider vinegar.

Ingredients

- Swiss chard
- Spinach
- Bok choy
- Collard greens
- Kale
- Carrots

Roast

Bake in the oven at 350°F until tender. Sprinkle with sea salt, herbs, and spices.

Ingredients

- Yams
- Sweet potatoes
- Red potatoes
- Squash
- Pumpkins
- Beets
- Brussels sprouts

ULTRA ENERGY BARS

Rich isn't the only one who loves the supercharged vitality he experiences from eating these nutritious homemade bars—our kids devour them as a healthy alternative to processed store-bought varieties. Power packed with healthy ingredients like nuts, seeds, coconut, and dried berries, these energy boosters boast a plentitude of protein, healthy fats, and fiber that will keep your engine revving all day long. Great for packing in your child's lunch box! Eat one of these bars and then, as Rich says, *get it done.*

Ingredients

- 1 cup raw almonds or walnuts, soaked overnight in filtered water
- ¼ cup cacao nibs
- ¼ cup hemp seeds
- ¼ cup dried goji berries
- 2 tablespoons cacao powder
- ¼ cup shredded coconut
- Pinch large-grain Celtic sea salt
- 7 or 8 dates, soaked in filtered water for 30 minutes and pitted

Preparation

1. In a food processor, pulse the nuts until mealy in texture.

2. Add the cacao nibs, hemp seeds, goji berries, cacao powder, coconut, and sea salt to the processor. Pulse again until well incorporated.

3. With the motor running, add one date at a time. After 7 dates, you will see the mixture ball up on one side of the bowl. You may need to redistribute the mixture and process it again to make sure the dates are mixed in.

4. On a piece of parchment paper, press the cookies in an even layer about ¼" thick.

5. With a knife, score out a grid of rectangular pieces approximately 2" x 3". If desired, press additional hemp seeds or shredded coconut on the surface.

6. Wrap in parchment paper or parchment bags. Take them out on a trail run, hike, or bike ride to sustain you throughout your training session! Keep in a glass cookie jar on your kitchen counter or in the fridge for up to a week—if they last.

2-4

CHIA SEED PUDDING

We credit chia seed pudding as one of the first dishes that helped our children make the shift to plant-based eating. There are many different versions of this superfood pudding. We present three delicious flavors here. Try to remember to soak your chia seeds overnight. But if you forget, no big deal—just stir them in water for a few minutes, until they become gelatinous. Packed with brain food, this cacao version is our family favorite—a true breakfast of champions!

Cacao

A great recipe to inspire plant-based eating in kids of all ages.

Ingredients

- ½ cup chia seeds
- Filtered water
- ¼ cup raw honey or maple syrup, or 4 dates, soaked and pitted
- 1 small avocado
- 1 tablespoon coconut oil
- 2 tablespoons cacao powder

Preparation

1. In a small bowl, soak the chia seeds in 2 cups filtered water; stir until they expand and become gelatinous, about 3 minutes.

2. In a separate bowl, soak the dates (if using) in filtered water for about 30 minutes.

3. To a food processor or Vitamix, add the avocado, coconut oil, honey or dates, and cacao powder. Pour in the chia seeds and their soaking water. Process or blend on high. Adjust the sweetness to taste.

4. Place in serving bowls and chill for 2 hours or devour immediately.

recipe continues >>

Banana

With its light and delicate banana flavor, this pudding also works great as a lunchtime dessert.

Ingredients

- ½ cup chia seeds
- 2 cups filtered water
- 1 ripe banana
- 1 tablespoon coconut oil
- ¼ cup raw honey
- 1 vanilla bean, split lengthwise, insides scraped out

Preparation

1. In a small bowl, soak the chia seeds in the filtered water and stir until they expand and become gelatinous, about 3 minutes.

2. To a food processor or Vitamix, add the banana, coconut oil, honey, and vanilla bean seeds. Pour in the chia seeds and their soaking water. Process or blend on high. Adjust the sweetness to taste.

3. Place in serving bowls and chill until cold or devour immediately.

Blueberry

During the height of local blueberry season, I created a version of this pudding my kids still talk about. But be careful—if you serve it with our Cashew Vanilla Cream (page 81), you may just experience ecstasy!

Ingredients

- ½ cup chia seeds
- 2 cups filtered water
- 2 pints fresh blueberries
- 1 teaspoon vanilla extract
- ¼ cup raw honey
- Cashew Vanilla Cream (page 81)

Preparation

1. In a small bowl, soak the chia seeds in the filtered water; stir them until they expand and become gelatinous, about 3 minutes.

2. To a food processor or Vitamix, add the blueberries, vanilla, and honey. Pour in the chia seeds and their soaking water. Process or blend on high. Adjust the sweetness to taste.

3. Transfer to a serving bowl and refrigerate for at least 2 hours. Serve with Cashew Vanilla Cream.

SUPERSOULFOOD PANCAKES

4

You can feel good about serving up a stack of these energy-rich pancakes. Chia, flax, and hemp seeds unite to pump up this pancake with superhero powers. Filled with healthy omega-3 EFAs, fiber, and protein, this dish is rocket fuel for your Plantpowered soul.

Ingredients

- 3 tablespoons ground flaxseeds
- 6 tablespoons plus 3¼ cups filtered water, plus more as needed
- 1 cup garbanzo flour
- 2 cups brown rice flour
- 2½ tablespoons potato starch
- 2 tablespoons baking powder
- 2 tablespoons chia seeds
- 2 tablespoons hemp seeds
- 1 teaspoon vanilla extract
- Zest of 1 lemon
- 2 tablespoons liquid coconut oil, plus more for grilling
- 2½ tablespoons sugar
- Maple syrup, to pour on top

Preparation

1. In a medium bowl, whisk the flaxseeds in 6 tablespoons of the filtered water until the consistency is "egg-like." Set aside.

2. In a large bowl, sift together the garbanzo flour, rice flour, potato starch, and baking powder. Using a wooden spoon, stir in the chia seeds and hemp seeds.

3. Add the vanilla, liquid coconut oil, remaining 3¼ cups water, and sugar to the flaxseed "egg" mixture. Make a well in the center of the dry mixture and fold in the wet mixture. Mix well.

4. Adjust your batter thickness by adding small amounts of filtered water.

5. Heat a cast-iron skillet and add coconut oil to lightly coat the pan.

6. Pour ¼ cup of the batter into the pan three times to make three pancakes. When bubbles have appeared throughout, flip them and cook on the opposite side for just a few minutes.

7. Serve the pancakes with rich organic maple syrup.

GETTING BACK TO THE ROOT

Sense & Sanity in Food and Lifestyle

To put it mildly, nutrition has become appallingly complicated. What should be elementary has become shamefully convoluted.

Low carb, high carb, slow carb. High fat, low fat, no fat. Zone and Blue Zone. Vegan, Paleo, Primal, Bulletproof, Mediterranean, Pritikin, Atkins, South Beach, Macrobiotic, Fruitarian, or Raw?

With so many choices, opinions, contradictory studies, and marketing hype surrounding what to eat, how much, and when, it's almost impossible to separate sense from insanity and fact from fiction.

Because the subject of diet is so emotionally charged—it's right up there with religion and politics—debating the merits of your favorite nutritional protocol all too often devolves into a counterproductive, never-ending, mudslinging merry-go-round. An unfortunate scenario that inflicts vertigo on even the most conscientious, label-reading consumer. And a big reason why the dreaded word *vegan* makes so many people recoil.

The only real beneficiaries of this confusion are the food and pharmaceutical industries. Fueled by politically powerful special interest groups that drive legislation, policy, and, ultimately, consumer choice, these humongous, well-funded conglomerates profit from our collective puzzlement to the tune of countless billions. Duping us into guzzling their nutritionally bankrupt fare of noxious yet highly addictive processed foods via hypnotic marketing tactics and misleading self-serving studies, the result is enslavement to deleterious eating habits that inevitably lead to a future of chronic illness. Not to mention an unfortunate yet costly long-term dependency on symptom-based medications just to keep us breathing.

The result? *Paralysis.* Perpetuation of our unhealthy yet culturally entrenched status quo. It's an insanity my friend John Joseph, author of *Meat Is for Pussies*, calls The Great Food Bamboozle.

Enough. The United States is the most prosperous nation on Earth. And yet we have never been more collectively unhealthy. It's shameful. I'm fed up. I hope you are, too.

So let's cut through the wide swath of confusion, misinformation, misdirection, marketing hype, and downright lies and get to the truth.

A truth so simple, it's been staring you in the face all along.

Let Plants Lead the Way

"Eat food. Not too much. Mostly plants."
—Michael Pollan, author of
The Omnivore's Dilemma

Although I would prefer that "Mostly" be supplanted with "Only," there is beauty in the simple straightforwardness of this profound proclamation.

To be sure, we can debate whether the human race is naturally omnivore or herbivore. But one cannot contend that we are *obligate* omnivores. I am living proof that the plant kingdom alone provides everything necessary to not only live but *thrive*.

This plant-centric approach to food and life will optimize your body weight. It will prevent and even reverse a vast array of the chronic diseases that have left us overweight and overmedicated. It will help put an end to our insane system of livestock agriculture that is decimating our ecology. The best part? You will achieve these results in a truly sustainable way by developing new habits with long-term staying power.

Simply put, eating plant-based is in the best interest of your long-term health *and* the future health of our planet—a planet that will soon perish if we refuse to innovate new and sustainable ways to feed the seven billion people and counting who currently walk the earth.

I'm not asking you to take my word for it. All I'm asking is that you suspend contempt prior to personal investigation. Set aside whatever preconceived opinions you may harbor. And when you are ready, take my hand. And let's give this plant-centric approach an honest try.

Here is some helpful information to guide your path.

Invest in Your Health

"Homicide is 0.8% of deaths. Diet-related disease is over 60%. But no one talks about it." —Jamie Oliver, celebrity chef

OK, so let's talk about it.

Heart Disease. America's number one killer. This epidemic is so pervasive, one out of every two Americans will develop some form of cardiovascular disease—50 *percent of the population!* In fact, one out of every three deaths is attributable this disease—33 *percent!* To put it into perspective, every twenty-five seconds an American suffers a coronary event. This disease alone costs us $109 billion a year in health care costs.

Obesity. Right now, 70 percent of the U.S. population is either obese or overweight. And childhood obesity rates have never been higher: 17 percent and rising. More than 12.5 million children in our country are fat and getting fatter, paving the way for a lifetime of illness, infirmity, and pharmaceutical dependence. Health care costs? $147 billion per year and escalating.

Type 2 Diabetes. When I was a kid, I don't think I knew anyone with this condition. Certainly not any young people. Now it's an epidemic. Estimates predict that by 2030, 50 percent of Americans will be diabetic or prediabetic!

This is just the tip of our heartbreaking health care crisis iceberg. And America is not alone in its suffering. Developing regions throughout China, India, and the Middle East are now experiencing unprecedented incidences of these diseases for the first time in the history of humankind. An expanding, global epidemic of vast proportions that can be directly pinpointed to the ascension of an international middle class clamoring to spend their newfound income on America's number one export—*unhealthy food.*

Insanity. There is no other way to say it.

The great irony is that these illnesses need never exist. Heart disease, obesity, diabetes, and countless other chronic infirmities all have one thing in common—they are all food-borne diseases. And they are all easily avoided through very simple diet and lifestyle alterations.

Adopting a plant-based diet is the true, sustainable path to disease prevention. In fact, eliminating animal products and processed foods from your plate is the single most impactful thing you can possibly do to stay on the right side of these dire statistics. So powerful, in fact, it can even reverse the onset of these and so many other debilitating infirmities that are unnecessarily killing our friends and family members.

Finally, it is imperative to understand that so many chronic illnesses that manifest later in life actually begin with unhealthy habits adopted during our formative years. So it's crucial that we develop new and better habits not only for ourselves but for our children. I'm not saying that getting your kids to eat right is always easy, only that its importance cannot be overstated—it's the best gift a parent can give a child.

Take a Stand for Our Planet

"You can't be an environmentalist, you can't be an ocean steward, without truly walking the walk. And you can't walk the walk in the world of the future—the world ahead of us, the world of our children—without eating a plant-based diet."
—James Cameron, Academy Award-winning filmmaker and environmentalist

Although it may come as some surprise, the true inconvenient truth is that raising animals for food is indisputably the single largest contributor to every environmental ill known to humankind: water scarcity, deforestation, land use, species extinction, ocean pollution, the destabilization of communities—and world hunger.

Bottom line? The world's obsession with an animal-centric diet is not only killing us, it's an environmental disaster that is polluting our atmosphere and waters, depleting our resources, obliterating species, and destroying the earth at a blinding rate of speed.

If we want to be healthy, stay healthy, and raise healthy, conscious children while simultaneously doing what is in the best long-term interest of the planet, then adopting a plant-based lifestyle isn't a choice, it's a mandate. It's the path to maximum, sustainable, long-term wellness and our collective responsibility as consumers, parents, and conscious stewards of the planet.

A more convenient truth is that by making a few simple dietary and lifestyle shifts, you need not participate in this cycle of lunacy.

Let's take a brief overview of what's really going on.

Water. In areas like California where drought is pervasive and water resources are precious, consumers are persistently reminded to conserve water resources by curtailing use. Hand-wash your dishes. Use eco-friendly, water-saving showerheads. Turn off the garden hose.

All good ideas, don't get me wrong. But focusing on consumer water consumption completely ignores the elephant in the room. The truth is that consumer water use accounts for only 5 percent of all U.S. water expenditures. By contrast, 56 percent of all U.S. water consumption is attributable to growing feed crops for livestock and quenching the thirst of animals specifically raised for human consumption.

The numbers are staggering. It requires more than 660 gallons of water just to produce a single quarter pound of hamburger. *You can save more water by not eating a pound of beef than you will save by not showering for eight months!*

Global Climate Change. Much like water, we as consumers are encouraged to reduce our oil and gas consumption, widely understood to be the primary contributor to global climate change. Ride your bike. Drive a hybrid. Or take the bus. But all transportation combined—including every car, airplane, bus,

and train on the planet—accounts for only 13 percent of total greenhouse gas emissions. By contrast, the 70 billion farmed animals walking the planet account for 51 percent of such greenhouse gas emissions worldwide.

Producing a single hamburger patty is the fossil fuel equivalent of driving a small car twenty miles and releases as much greenhouse gas into the atmosphere as driving that car nearly ten miles. In other words, ditching meat and dairy will have a far more profound impact on the environment than trading in your SUV for a Prius.

Species Extinction. As we speak, we are in the midst of the largest mass extinction of species since the dinosaurs disappeared off the planet sixty-five million years ago. The culprit? You guessed it. Due to overgrazing, habitat loss due to livestock overproduction, and the overfishing of our oceans, animal agriculture is the primary culprit when it comes to the irreparable vanishing of species from the face of the earth.

Deforestation. Our global rain forests are the planet's lungs—inhaling CO_2 and exhaling oxygen. Without them, the planet as we know it simply cannot survive. And yet we are decimating these precious resources at the rate of one acre—an entire football field—per second. This is a greenhouse gas emissions disaster that also results in the loss of close to a hundred plant, animal, and insect species *daily*!

Again, the driving force is animal agriculture. In fact, a full 91 percent of the loss of rain forests in the Amazon area is attributable to this industry, which requires massive amounts of ever-expanding landmasses to graze animals and grow feed for cows, pigs, chickens, and factory-farmed fish.

Our Oceans. We're all worried about the gelatinous garbage mass the size of Texas floating around somewhere in the Pacific. Plastic and trash flowing into our oceans is a huge problem, for sure. But even this pales in comparison to the deleterious effects of animal agriculture on the health of our oceans. Mass runoff due to livestock harvesting is by far our biggest oceanic polluter. Antibiotic-laden and disease-infested animal waste that seeps into our soil finds its way to our rivers, eventually flowing to our oceanic tributaries. The result is mass pollution in the form of giant "algal blooms" that gobble up the oxygen in the water, ultimately creating "dead zones"—thousands of square miles so oxygen deprived that aquatic life is rendered impossible.

Avoid GMO Foods

Defined by their scientifically engineered DNA, genetically modified organisms are primarily designed to render certain crops more robust and pest resistant. It sounds innocuous enough, positive even. But there is more at play.

The long-term health and environmental implications of GMO-based foods is the subject of much dispute. However, there is evidence to suggest a link between the ingestion of these foods and certain autoimmune disorders, infertility, gastrointestinal disorders, allergic reactions, and decreased antibiotic efficacy.

The most common GMO foods are soybeans, corn, and sugar beets. Unfortunately, the United States does not mandate that food manufacturers disclose the inclusion of GMOs on food labels. And you might be amazed to discover just how many food products—particularly processed snack foods—contain GMOs. This is a trend that is woefully underregulated and accelerating at a hyperbolic rate of speed, far eclipsing our ability to study, let alone understand, the long-term effects on human, animal, and environmental health. The best and only way to steer clear is to ensure to your foods are officially labeled organic.

Ditch Gluten

Hype or Reality? Going gluten-free is suddenly all the rage. But what is gluten? And is it truly harmful? In very basic terms, gluten is a sticky protein composite that is commonly found in a variety of grains—predominantly in wheat but also in barley, spelt, rye, and others.

Gluten is toxic to those who suffer from celiac disease. But recent years have seen a massive increase in non-celiac gluten intolerance, catalyzing a spectrum of insidious reactions caused by the inflammation-inducing effects of gluten ingestion. These include digestive problems, migraines, brain disorders, arthritis, fatigue, and infertility. Some research even supports a link between gluten intake and the expression of autism symptoms, as well as the onset of dementia.

But humans have been eating wheat forever—why is this happening now? Because today's wheat is not your grandmother's wheat. The hybridization of wheat crops over the last fifty years has decimated the nutritional value of this grain while simultaneously increasing gluten content exponentially. Moreover, there has been a massive increase in consumption, primarily due to our insatiable demand for wheat-based processed foods like bread, pasta, and crackers. The result? A spectrum of allergic reactions, ranging from mild to severe.

Gauge your level of sensitivity by eliminating gluten from your diet and monitoring your response. My personal opinion? We have become unnecessarily dependent upon grain in our diet. So minimize it to the best of your ability, or ditch it altogether and trade up with gluten-free whole grains like millet, buckwheat, amaranth, and sorghum.

Buy Organic & Local

Does it really matter? Yes. I could get into an entire dissertation on this subject, but the fact of the matter is that conventionally grown produce is rife with pesticides, herbicides, and GMOs. Because the roots of these plants absorb these chemicals into the cell walls of the plant itself, washing isn't enough. Invest in organic—you're worth it. The best option, particularly when it comes to further reducing your carbon footprint and supporting the organic farming movement, is to buy local whenever possible. Research local sustainable farms, co-ops, and farmers' market options— you just might be surprised by the opportunities available to you. Better yet—start growing your own food!

Let's Not Forget Compassion

We share this planet with our animal friends. In light of all the health and environmental reasons favoring an animal-free diet, it becomes impossible to reconcile the mass suffering caused by industrialized livestock agriculture—billions of animals raised in horrific conditions, fed unhealthy foods, pumped with antibiotics and hormones, restrained in cages or confined spaces, unnecessarily abused, inexcusably tortured, and ultimately slaughtered. Even the most hardened carnivore would agree that our system of factory farming is fundamentally inhumane.

I'm not asking you to become an animal lover if that's not your thing. Only to consider the broader implications inherent in the choices we make daily about what lands on our plate. We simply can no longer afford to turn a blind eye to the systems at play that drive consumer food choice.

As consumers we vote with our dollar. That money spent is a reflection of our values. So ask yourself this: *What am I voting for? Who am I and what do I truly stand for?*

Raise Your Vibration

We are all products of our environment. Everyone understands that if you sit in a dark room for too long, you become depressed. If you surround yourself with negative people, you will soon follow suit. But go to the beach on a sunny day, or immerse yourself in a group of energetic and enthusiastic friends, and suddenly you feel better.

Everything is energy. Food is no different. Just as the vibration of your surroundings can dictate mood, outlook, and behavior, so can your choices about how you feed yourself. Eat a heavy meal, a bag of processed pretzels, or a quart of ice cream and you will undoubtedly find yourself lethargic, even immobilized. But drink a kale smoothie, eat a quinoa salad or even just an orange, and you feel energized. This is not rocket science!

Food as fuel. You wouldn't put low-octane gas in an expensive sports car, so treat yourself with equal courtesy. You're far more valuable anyway! Food should nourish. Food should raise your vibration. And when done right—using recipes from this book and more—it can and will.

Baby Steps Move Mountains

Some people jump into this lifestyle with both feet and never look back. I applaud the commitment. For most, however, the transition is gradual. On a personal level, my evolution to a plant-based lifestyle was hardly overnight. I understand and empathize with a measured process of eliminating animal products and processed foods from your fridge and pantry.

A good place to start is swapping out your milk for plant-based alternatives derived from almond, coconut, or hemp. Push the meat entrée to a small side dish if you're not ready to completely let go. Instead of chicken wings, try a baked yam instead. You get the picture. The idea is to create new sustainable habits—one at a time, if necessary—that work within the construct of your busy life. Consistency is king. So focus on developing habits with staying power.

Embrace Imperfection

Just let it go. As you begin this journey, don't be surprised by a midnight ice cream lapse or an afternoon potato chip binge. I've been there. *To err is human,* as they say. The important thing is to understand that missteps are not mistakes, but rather opportunities to learn more about what drives the habits that don't serve you—the powerful emotional underpinnings of food addiction and cravings.

Rather than flog yourself over a slip, embrace it as simply an integral part of the process of change. Punish yourself and you've just made a second mistake—because holding yourself to an unrealistic standard, especially early on in your transition, is a pattern that can lead to defeatism. A shame spiral that can take you out of the game altogether. And the game is all about long-term sustainability over short-term temporary gains.

Slip up? Don't sweat it. Just make the next right choice. And when in doubt, **go back to the root**. Whole, plant-based foods prepared close to their natural state. This is the general rule of thumb that never fails.

It worked for me. And I promise it can work for you, too.

Don't Deprive—Thrive!

When the subject comes up about eating a plant-based diet, the focus inevitably turns to what you will miss, what is left out, what is lacking.

What am I going to do without my beloved cheese?

This is not about deprivation, suffering, or *lack*. Instead, it's about improving your health, increasing your vitality, and doing what's best not just for you but for all of us as one connected organism we call Earth.

So let's flip the equation. Shift perspective away from what is missing on your plate and let's focus on all the new, nutritious foods you are now *including*.

Look at it like an exhilarating adventure. Excitement over trying new things. Keep it light. And make it fun.

As you engage this shift, you will be amazed at how your palate will change. Feeding yourself with foods that actually nourish you, your energy levels will rise. Maintaining that good-feeling high vibration will begin to take precedence. Suddenly those irresistible cravings for so-called comfort foods will dissipate. And you will find yourself looking forward to meals that truly nourish.

I hear what you are saying. But I just can't imagine I will never again eat a steak.

Don't fall into this way of thinking—it's a mental trap. Avoid "absolutes" by staying rooted in the day, or even the moment if need be. Instead try this:

Maybe I will eat a steak tomorrow. But today—right now—I'm eating Julie's Raw Asian Salad. It tastes amazing. And I feel fantastic!

Conclusion

The solution is obvious. Eating plant-based will automatically help manage your weight. It will make you bulletproof to Western disease. It will conserve planetary resources. It will more than fuel whatever athletic pursuit you engage in. And it will even promote your children growing into more health and environmentally conscious citizens. All of these things serve the best interests of you, your family, and the planet at large.

Eating this way didn't just repair my health, it revitalized me wholesale. It even changed our family dynamic, creating deeper intimacy—bringing us closer as we congregate around the kitchen and table to share this voyage together.

Not only was it easier than I ever imagined, but I no longer crave the foods that once enslaved me. I look forward to my plant-based meals and can't imagine any other way.

So take my hand and let's make the leap. Together. Not only will you look and feel better, but you'll never look back.

So what are you waiting for?

SOUPS +
SALADS

WARM + COOL VIBRATIONS

I find that children and adults alike love eating soups. What is it about a warm, steaming bowl of goodness that provides the feeling that all is well? I think it's because it reminds us of the warmth and safety of a mother's care.

Soups are warming, nourishing bowls that carry a medley of high-vibration ingredients in bubbling, healing waters.

The secret trick to preparing delicious soups is to avoid over-cooking the veggies. In a large pot, first sauté the harder veggies such as carrots and celery. Then add your favorite spices to the mix. My typical rotation includes cumin, fresh ginger, and turmeric root. Now, add liquid and quickly blanch the greens and lighter veggies for no more than a few minutes. Kill the flame and let the flavors blend naturally. Add a simple squeeze of lemon. For more of a meal, serve the soup over steamed quinoa, buckwheat, millet, or rice. Always top it off with a nice garnish of fresh sprouts and seeds.

Salads are cooling, crunchy, and alive vibrations of "yum."

Eating raw greens and veggies deeply connects us to Mother Nature. Chewing these plants with mindful awareness gets our metabolism churning by signaling our bodies to begin the digestive process. I cannot overstate the extent to which regularly eating raw vegetable salads high in fiber and a wide array of essential vitamins, minerals, micronutrients, and phytonutrients is absolutely vital to maximum health. An added boost? All that roughage will clean you out by significantly easing the elimination of unwanted digestive waste buildup. As you begin to acclimate to this routine, focus on cutting down on or completely eliminating oily salad dressings and opt instead to grace your greens with zesty lemon juice, apple cider vinegar, or gluten-free tamari. If you want a bit of creamy goodness to accent your homemade dressing, add a bit of avocado or some blended cashews or Brazil nuts. And don't forget to experiment with fresh herbs!

BLACK BEAN SOUP

Our favorite bean is blended into a creamy, delightful bisque in this simple mix-and-go recipe that is great if you're short on time but don't want to compromise on taste. It's an affordable homemade soup that is nutritionally dense, delicious, and high in protein, dietary fiber, and complex carbohydrates. Garnish this sure-to-please, dark legume–based puree with fresh chopped cilantro to cleanse and heal your body.

Ingredients

- 2 cups drained black beans
- 2 cups black beans with liquid
- 2 garlic cloves
- 3 dehydrated sun-dried tomatoes, soaked for about 30 minutes
- 1 teaspoon cumin
- 1 teaspoon chili powder
- 1 teaspoon Celtic sea salt
- 1 tablespoon blue agave
- ½ cup fresh cilantro, chopped, for garnish
- Juice of 1 to 2 limes
- Brazil Nut Cream Spread (page 79)

Preparation

1. Add all the ingredients except the cilantro and lime juice to a Vitamix. Blend on high until the mixture is smooth.

2. Transfer to a saucepan, heat over medium-low heat, stir until warm, and adjust the seasonings to taste.

3. Garnish with the cilantro and a squeeze of lime juice.

4. We serve this with our Brazil Nut Cream Spread.

GINGER TURMERIC CARROT SOUP

A happy marriage of carrots and ginger, two root vegetables we love to taste together. This orange bowl of love is always harmonious and delicious. It is one of the first soups I learned to make as a young girl and I still remember how surprised I was to find it so incredibly easy! You can give this recipe a tropical flair by adding fresh mango, coconut, or orange. I like mine with a little touch of India, warmed with a hint of ginger and aromatic cumin. Loaded with beta-carotene, vitamins A, B, and C, and anti-inflammatory turmeric, this soup is a powerhouse of nutrition.

Ingredients

- 12 carrots
- 2 celery stalks with leaves
- 2" piece fresh ginger, peeled
- 1" piece fresh turmeric root, peeled
- 1 tablespoon coconut oil
- 8 cups filtered water
- Juice of 2 large oranges
- 1 teaspoon cumin
- 2 teaspoons Celtic sea salt
- Cracked black pepper, to taste

Preparation

1. Chop the carrots and celery into large rustic-size pieces. Grate the ginger and turmeric.

2. In a large, deep saucepan, heat the coconut oil over high heat, add the carrots, and sauté until the color brightens. Add the celery and sauté for a few minutes longer, just until the green color of the celery is enhanced.

3. Transfer the carrots, celery, and filtered water to a Vitamix or high-powered blender. Blend on high for a full 2 minutes.

4. Pour the blended mixture back into the saucepan.

5. Stir in the grated ginger and turmeric and add the orange juice. Simmer over low heat, stirring continuously.

6. Season with the cumin, sea salt, and pepper. Serve with our Veggie Burgers (page 199), Untuna Wraps (page 229) or Superfood Pad Thai (page 218).

Chef's Note: For a creamy twist, add ¼ cup fresh coconut meat or a 15-ounce can of coconut milk.

CLEANSING BEET SOUP

This soup embodies healing. It's the first recipe I go to whenever any one of us is feeling depleted. Our little girls have fallen in love with this soup and they miraculously eat all the beet greens! I think the secret is that splash of apple cider vinegar and that pinch of high-quality sea salt. If I am using it to heal a cold or reset my diet, I will use the garlic in this recipe for its detoxifying medicinal properties. The boys and Rich like to add a dash of cayenne for a spicy flair. It's also a great detox soup as the cilantro helps clear the body of heavy metals. Make it more of a meal by pouring it over some soft cooked quinoa or millet.

Ingredients

- 3 large fresh beets with beet greens
- 2 celery stalks
- 1 bunch fresh cilantro
- 1 tablespoon coconut oil
- 1 lime, halved
- 4 cups filtered water
- ¼ cup apple cider vinegar
- 2 garlic cloves (optional—for sickness or detox only)
- Celtic sea salt, to taste
- Dash cayenne pepper (optional)

Preparation

1. Wash the beets and remove the top and root. Leaving the skins on, slice the beets into 1" sections. Make sure they are small enough to fit onto a spoon but large enough that you feel their hearty flavor.

2. Wash the beet greens well and gather them into a bundle stacked on top of each other. Slice into 1" ribbon sections crosswise.

3. Wash the celery and chop into ½" pieces.

4. Wash the cilantro, gather in a bundle, and chop into ¼" pieces (including the stems). Make sure you can still see some whole cilantro leaves intact.

5. In a large pot, heat the coconut oil over medium heat.

6. Add the celery and sauté for a minute or two, until the color brightens.

7. Add the sliced beets and repeat. Squeeze the lime juice into the beets and celery and stir.

8. Add the water, apple cider vinegar, and garlic cloves (if sick or detoxing) and bring to a boil.

9. Add the beet greens and cilantro and simmer for only 3 minutes. Turn off the heat and adjust the seasonings with sea salt, apple cider vinegar, and cayenne (optional).

SPROUTED MUNG KICHERI

I had the honor of preparing this dish for the sacred *prasad* meal at a meditation event we hosted at our home. His Holiness Vidyadhishananda, a beloved Himalayan monk, gave it his blessing. This version of kicheri is fresh, crisp, and vibrant. It celebrates the cleansing tradition of this healing Indian dish while accentuating the fresh qualities of these delightful flavors. It's best if you sprout the mung beans, which will take a few days. The actual preparation of the stew is relatively quick and easy.

Ingredients

- 4 celery stalks
- 2 large carrots
- 2 tablespoons coconut oil
- 3 cups sprouted mung beans (see page 10)
- ¼ cup ground cumin
- Juice of 2 large lemons
- 6 cups filtered water
- ¼ cup grated fresh turmeric
- ¼ cup apple cider vinegar
- 2 teaspoons large-grain Celtic sea salt
- 1 bunch fresh cilantro

Preparation

1. Chop the celery and carrots into ¼" pieces.

2. In a large pot, heat the coconut oil over medium heat; add the carrots and sauté for approximately 3 minutes.

3. Add the celery and sauté until the color brightens. Add the sprouted mung beans and stir.

4. Now add the ground cumin and the juice from one of the lemons and stir until the veggies and beans are well coated.

5. Add the filtered water and simmer over medium heat for 20 minutes.

6. Add the grated turmeric, apple cider vinegar, the juice of the second lemon, and the sea salt.

7. Continue to simmer for another 10 minutes.

8. Adjust the seasoning to taste, adding a bit more apple cider vinegar, lemon juice, or sea salt.

9. Roughly chop the fresh cilantro, making sure some of the leaves are whole.

10. Just before serving, fold in the fresh cilantro.

TEMPEH CHILI

A Super Bowl favorite! Whether you're a sports fan or not, this recipe is something to cheer about. Truth be told, my son Trapper is the sole sports fan in our household. I know nothing about sports, so I make sure that at least I show up for the important games with some loving and supportive food for my boy! Trapper loves our fire-roasted tempeh chili at game time. Its smoky seasoning, fiber-filled black beans, and barbecue tempeh load the dish with a full-bodied, nourishing flavor. Super hearty, we serve it with our moist Zucchini Bread (page 130) and Roasted Corn & Tomato Salad (page 175). Follow it up with a dessert of Mexican Cacao Brownies (page 278).

Ingredients

- 4 cups dried black beans, or 8 cans black beans, drained and rinsed
- 2 garlic cloves, peeled and mashed
- 6¼ cups filtered water
- 2 (8-ounce) packages tempeh
- 1 (12-ounce) bottle high-quality barbecue sauce
- Brazil Nut Tomatillo Cream (page 103)
- 2 red bell peppers
- 1 medium apple (red or pink local variety)
- 3 tablespoons ground cumin
- 2 tablespoons raw cacao powder
- 2 tablespoons chili powder
- 1 tablespoon Celtic sea salt

Preparation

1. Soak the dried beans overnight or bring to a boil and let sit for a few hours prior to cooking.

2. In a large pot, cook the dried beans and garlic in 6 cups of the filtered water over medium heat until soft but not mushy. This could take up to 2 hours.

Alternatively, pour the canned beans into a large pot. Add the garlic and 6 cups of the filtered water and simmer over medium heat.

3. In a separate bowl, crumble the tempeh into small pieces, similar in consistency to taco meat. Pour the barbecue sauce over it and mix well. Set aside to marinate for an hour.

4. Make the Brazil Nut Tomatillo Cream.

5. Remove the tops from the peppers. Slice them open lengthwise, quarter them, and remove the seeds.

6. In a cast-iron skillet or wok, blacken the peppers over high heat. Transfer them to a cutting board and slice them into small chunks. Add them to the beans and stir.

7. Quarter, core, and seed the apple. Do not peel. Transfer the apple to a Vitamix or high-powered blender and add the remaining ¼ cup filtered water. Blend on high until the apple has been reduced to sauce. Pour it into the beans.

8. Add the crumbled tempeh to the hot, bubbling beans. Add the cumin, cacao powder, chili pepper, and salt. Simmer for 20 minutes to blend the flavors. Adjust the seasonings to your liking. Enjoy!

HEIRLOOM TOMATO SOUP

A love note to radiant skin, this cold soup is certain to shine on any table. Filled with sun-ripened tomatoes and other garden-fresh vegetables and vitamins, the soup will gift your body with nourishing minerals and antioxidants. If you use darker-colored greens or the browns and yellows typical of heirloom tomato varieties, it will look more like a mystery veggie stew. If you want it to read "tomato," bright red heirlooms work best.

Ingredients

- 6 large heirloom tomatoes in the color your prefer
- 2 celery stalks
- ¼ cup fresh purple basil
- ¼ cup fresh green basil
- ¼ cup fresh mint
- 1 teaspoon celery seed
- 2 tablespoons high-quality olive oil
- 1 teaspoon Celtic sea salt
- 1 lemon
- Cracked black pepper, to taste

Preparation

1. Slice the heirloom tomatoes into quarters.

2. Chop the celery in large chunks, making sure to include the leaves.

3. Remove the leaves from the stalks of the purple and green basil as well as the mint. Reserve some sprigs for garnish.

4. In a food processor, add the tomatoes, celery, celery seed, olive oil, and fresh herbs. Pulse intermittently and deliberately until the mixture reaches a slightly chunky consistency. Be careful not to over-process or your soup will be watery.

5. Add the sea salt, a squeeze of lemon, and some pepper. Adjust the seasoning to taste.

Chef's Note: If you use farmer-grown heirlooms, this soup should be served raw. If you want to use other varieties of tomatoes, slightly blacken them first in a cast-iron pan using no oil.

RED CHARD MISO SOUP

Ribbons of chard and chopped cilantro decorate this colorful and healing bowl. It's one of our favorites to enjoy around a fire. It's also a great replacement for Mom's chicken soup when you need to regain your balance. The key to this great soup is to only slightly cook the veggies. If you do not overcook, the entire soup should be ready in fifteen minutes. The apple cider vinegar gives great flavor to the mix. Featuring a bounty of healthy vegetables, this nourishing pot is sure to make everyone feel their best. Get adventurous and create your own variety by switching up the vegetables.

Ingredients

- 8 ounces udon noodles or gluten-free rice noodles
- 1 package small brown cremini mushrooms
- 1 teaspoon sesame oil
- ½ cup chopped green onions
- Small bunch red chard, cut into 1" strips
- 4 tablespoons apple cider vinegar
- 4½ cups filtered water
- ½ cup yellow miso
- Juice of 1 lemon
- 2 tablespoons namah shoyu
- 1 bunch fresh cilantro, chopped
- Pinch Celtic sea salt

Preparation

1. In a medium pot, boil water and cook the udon according to the package directions. Drain and set aside.

2. Wash and stem the mushrooms. In a large soup pot, sauté the mushrooms in the sesame oil over medium heat.

3. Add the green onions and stir for 30 seconds.

4. Add the chard and stir again for 30 seconds.

5. Add 2 tablespoons of the apple cider vinegar and stir again. Then quickly add 4 cups of the filtered water. You want the veggies warmed but still bright in color.

6. In a separate small bowl, mix the miso and the remaining ½ cup water; using a whisk or a fork, whisk the miso until smooth.

7. Add the lemon juice and namah shoyu to the miso mixture and whisk again. Then whisk the entire mixture into the pot with the veggies and simmer for 5 minutes.

8. Add the udon and cilantro. Add the remaining 2 tablespoons vinegar and a sprinkle of sea salt. Adjust the seasonings to taste. Enjoy!

WARM MUSHROOM SALAD

As the saying goes, variety is the spice of life. Variety should also be the hallmark of the salads we put on our table. This recipe is inspired by a beautiful memory of picking *champignons* in the forest of Normandy. Having this warm, earthy mushroom element in a salad makes for a very satisfying lunch entrée. When I am making mushroom dishes, I always try to source a wonderful variety basket from a local farmer. Farm-fresh sprouts boost the vitality of this dish and provide your body with healing nourishment.

Ingredients

- 2½ cups farmers' market mushrooms
- 1 tablespoon macadamia nut oil or olive oil
- Juice of 1 lemon
- Celtic sea salt
- Classic Dijon Honey Dressing (page 112)
- 1 head butter lettuce
- ½ cup raw walnuts
- 1 sprig fresh thyme
- 1 bunch fresh sunflower sprouts

Preparation

1. Wash the mushrooms and remove the stems. Chop them in large rustic-style sections, preserving the natural forms of the varieties.

2. In a cast-iron skillet or wok, heat the oil on medium and sauté the mushrooms until their juices release. Turn off the heat, squeeze the lemon juice over the mushrooms, and stir. Sprinkle with sea salt.

3. In the bottom of a large salad bowl, prepare the Classic Dijon Honey Dressing.

4. Tear the head of butter lettuce into bite-size pieces and add to the large salad bowl. Add the mushrooms. Sprinkle in the walnuts and fresh thyme. Toss just before serving.

5. Garnish with a bunch of fresh sprouts.

PARISIAN ASPARAGUS SALAD OO LA LA . . .

When I was living in Paris during my college days, my dear friend Sofie taught me how to make proper Dijon dressing. The thing I loved most about Sofie's technique was that she prepared the dressing in the bottom of the serving bowl and would wait to toss the salad until just before serving. This way the lettuce always stays crisp. From that day forward I've used this approach with nearly every salad I make, thinking of her fondly each and every time. Sometimes I wonder, is she thinking of me?

Ingredients

- 1 bunch asparagus
- 2 to 4 Yukon Gold, fingerling, or red potatoes
- 1 bunch shelf mushrooms
- 1 tablespoon walnut or olive oil
- 1 lemon
- Celtic sea salt
- 1 medium endive
- 2 tablespoons fresh chives
- 2 sprigs fresh dill
- Classic Dijon Honey Dressing (page 112)
- 6 cups mesclun spicy mix lettuce or baby arugula
- ½ cup capers
- Crumbled Walnut Parmesan (page 78), for garnish

Preparation

1. Rinse the asparagus. In a large, deep saucepan, arrange the asparagus in a single layer and cover with about 1" of water. Over medium heat, boil the asparagus until tender. Cut into ½" pieces, making sure to preserve the spears. Discard the tough ends of the stems. Set aside.

2. Wash the potatoes, taking care to scrub off any soil. In a medium pan, boil the potatoes until tender. Drain and cut into ½" pieces. Set aside.

3. Wash the mushrooms and cut off the stems. Using your hands, tear the mushrooms into smaller pieces. In a medium saucepan, sauté the mushrooms in the walnut oil until their juices release. Turn off the heat and squeeze a lemon over the top. Sprinkle with sea salt and set aside.

4. Slice the endive into ⅛"-thick pieces. Pull apart the sections to reveal its delicate rings. Chop the chives and the dill.

5. In the bottom of a large salad bowl, prepare the Classic Dijon Honey Dressing. Add the asparagus and potatoes. Toss to coat.

6. Add the mesclun salad, capers, endive, and fresh herbs. Toss.

7. Use the Crumbled Walnut Parmesan to garnish the salad. Serve.

RAW BOK CHOY, SHELF MUSHROOM & MUNG BEAN SALAD

This is a great raw salad to serve with any Asian-style dish. Similar to kale, if the bok choy is cut into thin pieces and massaged with dressing, the bitterness and texture soften, making for a quick and easy dinner salad. With fresh colors and flavors, this combination is filled with essential nutrients, protein, vitamins, and minerals. To look and feel your best, create this crunchy salad today and feel the power of raw food work magic in your life.

Ingredients

- 4 heads bok choy
- Asian Dressing (page 115)
- 1 bunch shelf mushrooms (about 1 cup)
- 2 cups mung bean sprouts
- 1 red bell pepper, seeded and diced

Preparation

1. Wash the bok choy well. Cut off the bottom stem pieces. Then slice the leaves into ¼"-inch sections. Set aside.

2. In a medium bowl, whisk together the Asian Dressing ingredients. Add the sliced bok choy.

3. Massage the dressing into the bok choy, thinking good thoughts and healing intentions.

4. Add the mushrooms, mung bean sprouts, and bell pepper. Toss and enjoy!

GRILLED VEGGIE SALAD

Summer on a plate, this very hearty mix makes a lovely main dish during the warmer months. The combination of crisp lettuce leaves and Dijon-marinated blackened vegetables are a wonderful juxtaposition of flavors and textures. Seasonal garden-fresh veggies are a great way to brighten up the dish and increase your family's enjoyment of nourishing plants.

Ingredients

- 2 ears corn
- 2 red bell peppers
- 2 zucchini, cut into ½" spears
- 2 yellow squash, cut into ½" spears
- 1 red onion, cut into ½" slices
- A double batch of Classic Dijon Honey Dressing (page 112)
- Celtic sea salt, to taste
- Dash cayenne
- 1 head field lettuce, washed and dried
- 1 head romaine lettuce, washed and dried
- 1 bunch fresh dill, chopped
- Juice of 1 lemon, to taste

Preparation

1. In a cast-iron skillet or wok using no oil, blacken the ears of corn over high heat. Set aside.

2. Cut the peppers in quarters and remove the stems and seeds. Blacken the peppers, turning them until all sides are well charred. Set aside and repeat with the zucchini and squash spears. Finally, blacken the onion slices and remove from the heat.

3. In a large salad bowl, prepare the dressing.

4. Add sea salt and cayenne pepper to taste.

5. Place one ear of corn inside the bowl standing on end. Cut off the kernels using a downward motion. Rotate the cob until all the kernels are removed. Repeat with the other ear of corn.

6. Dice the red pepper, zucchini, and squash into small chunks. Dice the blackened onion slices into bite-size pieces.

7. Using your hands, fold the warm veggies into the dressing and set aside, allowing them to soak up the flavor of the dressing.

8. Tear the washed lettuces into bite-size pieces and add on top of the veggies.

9. Add the chopped fresh dill.

10. Toss just before serving.

11. Add the lemon juice. Adjust the seasoning to taste.

RAW KALE SALAD

Still not sure what to do with all that kale? Here's a refreshing way to add more to your plate. This is a super tasty raw salad that makes for a great lunch entrée or healthy side salad at dinnertime. Paired with carrots, beets, and crunchy heart-healthy walnuts, it's wonderfully colorful and incredibly good for you. Among kale's many benefits, its high level of vitamin K works with calcium to support the processes necessary to build strong bones. And beets are wonderful blood cleansers. *Kalelujah!*

Ingredients

- Asian Dressing (page 115)
- 2 bunches curly kale, washed, stems removed
- 1 raw beet
- 1 carrot
- ½ cup raw walnuts
- 1 lemon

Preparation

1. Prepare the Asian Dressing, whisking all the dressing ingredients together in the bottom of a large salad bowl.

2. Tear the kale leaves into bite-size pieces and add half of the kale to the salad bowl.

3. Using your hands, start massaging the kale to work the dressing into the leaves. The dressing will tenderize the leaves and the kale will reduce in size. As the kale relaxes, add the remainder of the kale leaves and massage once again.

4. Peel and wash the beet and carrot. Using a grater or a spiral veggie machine, grate or spiral them right into the kale mixture.

5. Add the walnuts and toss. Add a squeeze of lemon. Serve!

ROASTED CORN & TOMATO SALAD

Rich and I so enjoyed our travels in Chile that we can't wait to find an excuse to go back. Rich feels that one fantastic reason to return is that they have the largest swimming pool in the world. Many athletes would agree! Another great reason is the abundance of beautiful, natively grown farm-fresh fruit and veggies. Corn and tomatoes are a staple of many lunch and evening meals in my mother's native country. This recipe is a love note to my beautiful Chilean cousin Claudia who is spreading the Plantpower message all across Santiago. Do yourself a favor and splurge on high-quality heirloom tomatoes. I purposely cut them on the larger side so I can enjoy the succulent texture and sweet juicy bites. I'm happy to share a small piece of my heritage in this salad with hopes to inspire your next trip to Chile!

Ingredients

- 3 ears corn
- 1 tablespoon olive oil
- Juice of 1 lemon
- Celtic sea salt
- 3 ripe heirloom tomatoes
- ¼ cup pittted Spanish green olives
- 2 celery stalks with leaves, chopped
- 1 head butter lettuce
- Basil ribbons, for garnish
- Cracked black pepper

Preparation

1. Remove the corn kernels from the cobs by cutting them lengthwise.

2. In a wok over high heat using no oil, roast the corn kernels until slightly blackened. Set aside.

3. In a large salad bowl, combine the olive oil, lemon juice, and sea salt; whisk well and adjust the seasonings, adding more sea salt or lemon if needed.

4. Quarter the tomatoes. Chop the olives and the celery. Add them to the bowl with the dressing and toss.

5. Tear the lettuce leaves into bite-size pieces and add to the bowl. Top with the cooked corn. Toss once more.

6. Garnish with basil and cracked black pepper.

Regio!

SPINACH BEET SALAD

A fresh, nourishing summer salad that's sure to please. The combination of vegetables and toasted almonds accented with a sweet honey vinaigrette really makes these flavors pop. High in antioxidants, vitamins, and minerals, spinach also brims with disease-preventing phytonutrients. I love the fennel against the sweetness of the beets. You could also add sweet grapefruit or ripe oranges for a fun citrusy twist. Enjoy!

Ingredients

- 3 raw beets
- ½ cup raw almonds
- 2 endives
- ½ bulb fennel
- ½ cup fresh mint, plus more for garnish
- 4 cups baby spinach, washed
- Classic Dijon Honey Dressing (page 112)

Preparation

1. Wash the beets and remove the greens and the roots.

2. In a deep pot, boil the beets in water until tender (about 30 minutes). They should be soft when you stick a fork into the center.

3. Remove the beets and drain in a colander.

4. With the cold water running over the beets, remove the skins by rubbing them off with your fingers. Transfer the beets to a cutting board and dice into small pieces.

5. Preheat the oven to 325°F. On a cookie sheet, arrange the almonds in a thin layer and toast them in the oven for 10 minutes.

6. Chop the endive, making sure to remove the hard center piece. Do the same with the fennel bulb.

7. Chop the mint, reserving a few leaves for garnish.

8. In a large salad bowl, combine the washed spinach, endive, fennel, and mint. Place the beets on top.

9. Prepare the Classic Dijon Honey Dressing by putting all the dressing ingredients into a sealed jar and shaking well.

10. Pour the dressing over the salad and toss. Garnish with toasted almonds and mint.

KALE RADISH CELERY SALAD

This is a bright, crispy salad that is perfect for a main lunch course or as a side salad for the dinner meal. Radishes work as cleansers and detoxifiers, while kale infuses the dish with copious amounts of healthy antioxidants known as carotenoids and flavonoids. Optimize the many benefits of kale by massaging it with loving intentions. *Remember: thoughts are things!* Indeed, we are what we eat. But we are also what we think. Always look for creative ways to breathe more love and compassion into the meals you prepare.

Ingredients

- Grapefruit Miso Dressing (page 114)
- ½ bunch curly kale
- ½ bunch dinosaur kale
- 2 celery stalks
- 3 radishes

Preparation

1. In a serving bowl, whisk together the Grapefruit Miso Dressing ingredients and adjust the seasoning to taste.

2. Strip the curly kale from the stems and tear the leaves into bite-size pieces roughly 2" across.

3. Slice the dinosaur kale crosswise into small 1"-wide ribbons.

4. Put all the kale leaves into the bowl with the dressing. Using your hands, massage the kale until the dressing begins to tenderize and soften the leaves.

5. Dice the celery stalks, including the leaves. Slice the radishes into thin pieces.

6. Add the celery and the radishes to the bowl. Toss and serve!

POTATO SALAD

Summer cookouts and potato salad go hand in hand. Our version of this American favorite is sure to win you over. With fresh vibrant herbs, fresh olives, and powerful pumpkin seeds filled with protein and iron, this salad says ... *yes, let's eat outside!*

Ingredients

- 5 pounds red potatoes
- 1 cup Vegenaise
- ¼ cup Dijon mustard
- 2 tablespoons olive oil
- 2 teaspoons large-grain Celtic sea salt, plus more to taste
- 1 cup pitted Kalamata olives
- ¼ cup chopped fresh dill
- Fresh dill sprigs
- ¼ cup pepitas

Preparation

1. Wash the potatoes well, scrubbing the skins to remove any soil.

2. In a large pot of water, boil the potatoes over high heat until soft but not mushy. The potatoes are done when a fork slides easily into the center of the potatoes without breaking them apart.

3. Pour the potatoes into a colander and drain. If you wish to remove the skins, run a small stream of cold water over the potatoes and rub the skins off using your thumbs and fingers. Rich prefers I leave the skins on. This gives the dish a nutrient boost and enhances the hearty, country-style vibe.

4. In a large serving bowl, whisk together the Vegenaise, Dijon, and olive oil.

5. Using a knife, cut the warm potatoes crosswise and lengthwise into roughly ½" pieces and let them fall into the bowl with the dressing. Do this quickly; don't sweat precision. Keep cutting in all directions until all the potato slices are approximately ½" in size.

6. Using a large spoon, start turning the potatoes into the dressing at the bottom of the bowl. Continue until the mixture is well incorporated.

7. Add the sea salt and mix again. Add the olives and the chopped dill. Turn over again until well combined. Adjust the seasonings to taste.

8. Garnish with dill sprigs and pepitas and serve!

HULA KALE SALAD

I had the honor of serving as head chef at a yoga retreat on the sacred island of Kauai. There is a reason Kauai is dubbed the garden isle—it's truly a whole-food utopia. Harvesting plants directly from the rich red soil made every meal a feast of health and life. This Hawaiian salad emerged from the creative flow of that experience. A flowery work of art, I like to think it embodies the tradition and essence of the beautiful hula dance itself. Dance your way around the kitchen to create this buttery tropical delight!

Ingredients

- Asian Dressing (page 115)
- 2 large bunches curly kale
- 2 medium beets
- ¼ cup raw coconut
- 15 hibiscus or edible flowers (optional)
- 2 tablespoons hemp seeds
- 1 cup raw macadamia nuts

Preparation

1. Prepare the Asian Dressing by whisking the ingredients in the bottom of a large wooden bowl.

2. Add the kale leaves. Massage with your hands and the spirit of Aloha.

3. Using a spiral veggie slicer, spiral the beets into long, thin, delicate threads. Set aside.

4. Grate the raw coconut on a small grater into a small bowl. Set aside. Wash the flowers gently (if using) and pat dry with a towel.

5. Dust the kale with the coconut shavings and hemp seeds. Sprinkle in the macadamia nuts. Gently arrange the beet spirals and the flowers on top.

CABBAGE BEET GINGER SLAW

A coleslaw upgrade, this is a great fresh slaw to serve on a picnic or as a side to our Veggie Burgers (page 199). It also goes nicely with One Bowls (page 197). Filled with the power of root vegetables and fresh ribbons of cabbage, this is a crunchy, citrusy salad to serve with love. High in fiber, cabbage purifies the blood and soothes the nervous system while boosting energy. Reward your body with this amazing salad—*you deserve it!*

Ingredients

- ¼ cup apple cider vinegar
- 6 tablespoons namah shoyu
- Juice of 2 lemons
- Celtic sea salt, to taste
- 2" piece fresh ginger
- 4 raw beets
- 6 carrots
- 1 head Chinese cabbage or napa cabbage

Preparation

1. Add the apple cider vinegar, namah shoyu, lemon juice, and sea salt to the bottom of a large bowl.

2. Grate the ginger, beets, and carrots right into the bowl, leaving the skins on. Toss to coat.

3. Discarding any thick stem sections, slice the cabbage into very thin ribbons. Select the best 2 cups of cabbage leaf ribbons and add them to the bowl. Using your hands, toss until all the ingredients are well incorporated. Think happy thoughts.

4. Adjust the seasonings to taste.

RAW ASIAN SALAD

We love this raw salad brimming with Plantpowered whole foods! The secret to creating a gorgeous thoughtful presentation is using a spiral slicer (see page 34). Worth the extra effort, this salad is a bowl full of love. It is overflowing with vitamins and minerals and has a tangy mix of bright colors and flavors with a satisfying crunch. The little ones love to help spiral. Invite them to help create beautiful coiled veggie necklaces to adorn the rim of your salad bowl! Veggies are like life—it's all about how you slice it.

Ingredients

- Asian Dressing (page 115)
- 1 bunch shelf mushrooms
- 2 carrots
- 2 beets
- 2 cucumbers
- 1 (1-ounce) package sea vegetables
- 2 cups sprouted long-stem mung beans
- 1 (5-ounce) bag organic field spring lettuce mix
- 1 cup daikon sprouts

Preparation

1. In a large, beautiful serving bowl, whisk together all the Asian Dressing ingredients. Add the shelf mushrooms and let marinate for 30 minutes.

2. Using a spiral slicer, spiral the carrots, beets, and cucumbers.

3. Add the sea veggies and sprouted mung beans and toss to coat them well.

4. Add the lettuce and toss just before serving. Garnish with the carrot, beet, and cucumber spirals and bunches of daikon sprouts. Enjoy!

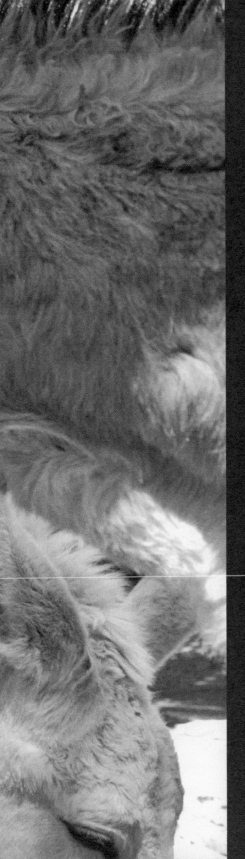

CHEW ON THIS!

THE "WAY" TO VIBRANT HEALTH . . .

If you are in the early stages of being Plantpowered, you may feel so amazing drinking juices and blends that you never want to eat real food again! But we're here to bring you back down to earth. Chewing your food is an essential part of digestion. During this process you are signaling to your body that it's time to begin breaking down foods so your body can assimilate the nutrients it needs. If you drink all your meals forever, you will be missing the highest healing combination: nutrients plus *prana*—the Sanskrit term for life force. So eat as many whole foods in their original state as you can. Gather the family around a beautiful table at least once a day and mindfully chew your way to vibrant health!

BUT WHERE DO YOU GET YOUR PROTEIN?

Eating Lower on the Food Chain: A Plea for Sanity

I am plant-based. Essentially, this means I don't eat anything with a face or a mother. Let's just say animals find this agreeable.

I'm also an ultra-endurance athlete. Essentially, this means I don't go all that fast, but I can go all day. Let's just say Julie finds this agreeable.

Conventional wisdom is that "vegan" and "athlete" simply don't get along. Let's just say it's irreconcilable differences. This is utter nonsense.

"But where do you get your protein?"

Not a day goes by that I am not asked this question. If I had a dollar for every time this came up, I could put all four of our kids through college.

Most vegans bristle at the question. Armed for battle, they assume an air of condescending, ethical superiority and hunker down for the age-old omnivore-versus-herbivore fight that almost inevitably ensues.

I hate that—it's why a large portion of the general public all too often finds the vegan rhetoric unpalatable.

Instead, I welcome the question. If someone is asking, I presume a genuine interest, simply an opportunity for a productive dialogue.

So let's try to have that dialogue. The productive kind. My perspective on the elephant in the room—nothing more, nothing less.

We live in a society in which we have been willfully misled to believe that meat and dairy products are the sole source of dietary protein worthy of merit. *Without copious amounts of animal protein, it's impossible to be healthy, let alone perform as an athlete*. The message is everywhere—from a recent (and wildly successful, I might add) high-profile dairy lobby ad campaign pushing chocolate milk as the ultimate athletic recovery beverage (diabolically genius) to compelling food labels to a dizzying array of fitness expert testimonials. Protein, protein, protein—generally reinforced with the adage that more is better.

Whether you are a professional athlete or a couch potato, this hardened notion is so deeply ingrained into our collective belief system that to challenge its propriety is nothing short of heresy. But through direct experience, I have come to believe that this pervasive notion is at best misleading, if not altogether utterly false, fueled by a well-funded campaign of disinformation perpetuated by powerful and well-funded BigFood, BigAg industrial animal agriculture interests that have spent countless marketing dollars to convince society that we absolutely need these products in order to breathe air in and out of our lungs.

Chances are that if you're reading this book, your mind is open to the idea that there is another way to eat.

The animal-protein push is not only based on lies; it's killing us, luring us to feast on a rotunda of factory-farmed, hormone- and pesticide-infused foods generally high in saturated fat, which—despite the current populist fervor over high-fat, low-carb diets—I remain convinced is indeed a contributing factor to our epidemic of heart disease (the developed world's number one killer) and many other Western diet- and lifestyle-induced infirmities that have rendered our prosperous nation one of the sickest societies on Earth.

Indeed, protein is an essential nutrient, absolutely critical not just for building and repairing muscle tissue, but in the maintenance of a wide array of important bodily functions. But does it matter if our protein comes from plants rather than animals? And how much do we actually need?

Proteins consist of twenty different amino acids, eleven of which can be synthesized naturally by our bodies. The remaining nine—what we call *essential amino acids*—must be ingested from the foods we eat. So technically, our bodies require certain amino acids, not protein per se. But these nine essential amino acids are hardly the exclusive domain of the animal kingdom. In fact, they're originally synthesized by plants and are found in meat and dairy products only because these animals have eaten plants. Despite the "butter is back" hysteria that recently graced the cover of *Time* magazine, the best medical science establishes beyond reproach that both casein and whey contribute materially to degenerative disease. A family of proteins found in milk, casein has been linked to the onset of a variety of diseases, including cancer. And whey is nothing more than a highly processed, low-grade discard of cheese production—another diabolical stroke of genius courtesy of the dairy industry that created a zillion-dollar business out of stuff previously tossed in the garbage.

On a personal anecdotal level, adopting a plant-based lifestyle eight years ago repaired my health wholesale and revitalized my middle-aged self to reengage fitness in a new way. As hard as it may seem to believe, the truth is that my athletic accomplishments were achieved not in spite of my dietary shift but rather as a direct result of adopting this new way of eating and living.

I'm not alone in this belief. Just ask Indianapolis Colts wide receiver Griff Whalen, Oakland Raiders defensive tackle David Carter, or strongman Patrik Baboumian, whom I personally witnessed break a World Record for most weight carried by a human being when he hauled more than 1,200 pounds—roughly the weight of a Smart Car— 10 meters across a stage in Toronto a few summers ago. There's my friend Timothy Shieff, parkour artist extraordinaire and two-time Freerunning World Champion, who defies gravity hopscotching off rooftops like a video-game character. Check out freak-of-nature strength athlete Frank Medrano, who can do things with his body you didn't think possible. Then there are MMA/UFC fighters like Mac Danzig, Jake Shields, and James Wilks. Multisport athletes like Brendan Brazier, Rip Esselstyn, and Ben Bostrom—a world-renowned motorcycle, mountain, and road bike athlete, victorious as a member of this year's Race Across America four-man relay team; professional triathlete and Ultraman World Champion Hillary Biscay, who recently raced her sixty-sixth Ironman; ultramarathoner extraordinaire Scott Jurek, his fruitarian compadre Michael Arnstein, and my EPIC5 compadre Jason Lester, who has crisscrossed the USA on two feet and recently completed a hundred-day run across China. Then of course there is boxer Timothy Bradley Jr., who (technically) took down Manny Pacquiao in 2012.

The point is this: each of these athletes, and countless others, will tell you the same thing: rather than steak, milk, eggs, and whey supplements, opt instead to eat lower on the food chain and source your protein needs from healthy non-inflammatory plant-based sources such as black, kidney, pinto, and other beans; almonds; lentils; hemp seeds; spirulina; and quinoa. Even eating less concentrated sources of protein like potatoes, sweet potatoes, and bananas will get you exactly where you need to be.

Even if you ate nothing but fruit, you *still* would never suffer a protein deficiency (or even any particular amino acid deficiency). Short of starving yourself, it's basically impossible.

Despite the incredibly heavy tax I impose on my body, training at times upwards of twenty-five to thirty hours per week for ultra-endurance events, this type of regimen has fueled me for years without any issues with respect to building lean muscle mass. In reality, I believe eating plant-based has significantly enhanced my ability to expedite physiological recovery between workouts—the holy grail of athletic performance enhancement. In fact, I can honestly say that at age forty-eight, I am fitter than I have ever been, even when I was competing as a swimmer at a world-class level at Stanford in the late 1980s.

And despite what you might have been told, I submit that more protein isn't better. Satisfy your requirement and leave it at that. With respect to athletes, to my knowledge no scientific study has ever shown that consumption of protein beyond the RDA-advised minimum (10 percent of daily calories) stimulates additional muscle growth or expedites physiological repair induced by exercise stress. And yet most people—the overwhelming majority of whom are predominantly sedentary—generally consume upwards of three times the amount of daily protein required to thrive.

The protein craze isn't just an unwarranted, overhyped red herring; it's harmful. Not only is there evidence that excess protein intake is often stored in fat cells, it contributes to the onset of a variety of diseases such as osteoporosis, cancer, impaired kidney function, and heart disease.

Still not convinced? Consider this: some of the fiercest animals in the world—the elephant, rhino, hippo, and gorilla—are Plantpowered herbivores. And nobody asks them where they get their protein. So ditch that steak and join me for a bowl of quinoa and lentils.

I encourage everyone reading this to take a leap of faith and give our healing recipes a try; I truly hope this book educates and inspires you to take your nutrition, health, and fitness to the next level. All as a means to help you unlock and unleash your best, most authentic self.

MAINS +
SIDES

IS IT A MAIN OR A SIDE?

You might think that waving good-bye to meat suddenly restricts your mealtime options. *In order to thrive, I must deprive.* But this is an old way of thinking. In truth, breaking away from the tired "meat protein entrée with a small vegetable side" paradigm liberates the creative imagination to invert and expansively redefine the unwritten rules that govern what a meal can and should look like.

What was once a "side" is now
a "main." What was once a "main"
is now a "side." It's time to have fun,
break a rule or two, and play!

In this section, you'll find a delicious diversity of hearty and robust recipes to perfectly accompany your salads and soups—just don't pigeonhole them into categories! Did I lose you? Sure, our Vegan Lasagna (page 236) can be served as a traditional main course, but it also makes a perfect side to our Cauliflower Mashed Potatoes (page 225). Tamales can be a main but also sing as a side dish to our Torre de Nachos (page 207).

When it comes to mealtime combinations, we encourage unbridled creativity in your selections. In fact, we encourage you to be *outrageous!*

ONE BOWLS

Creating a one-bowl meal is a really great way to get nourished and healthy. We go through stretches in our house when these are coming out of the kitchen on a daily basis for weeks on end. Primarily macrobiotic, they are a staple in our household and they keep our teenage boys fueled and happy. These dishes are made up of five general categories of ingredients: a legume, a grain, a green, a whole food, and a sauce. The possibilities are endless! Most of the elements can be made ahead of time so assembly takes just minutes. Use sprouted beans to lift the nutritional value. We love using our Fermented Probiotic Kraut (page 109) as a garnish to these hearty, well-balanced, and delicious meals. One bowls—perfect for lunch or dinner.

LAYER ON THE LEGUMES

- Black beans
- Adzuki beans
- Mung beans

All of these bean varieties will easily sprout over a 3-day period. I like to make a fresh pot of cooked sprouted beans and store them in the fridge for up to 3 days. Make sure you rinse the cooking water from the mung beans so they don't become pasty. Adding a large piece of kombu or raw seaweed to your pot will add great flavor and nutrients to your beans. Also adding in the Mexican herb asafoetida, turmeric, ginger, or black pepper helps manage gas with beans. Never add salt during the cooking process. Instead sprinkle a large-grain Celtic variety over the top of your meal just before you eat it.

GOOD GRAINS

- All colors of quinoa
- Millet
- Short-grain brown rice
- Exotic black or red rice
- Kelp noodles (grain substitution)

My first choice is quinoa: a high-protein seed. It's easier to digest than grains and packed with nutrition. Millet is low on the glycemic index and a fantastic multi-purpose, gluten-free grain. However, short-grain brown rice is also nourishing. Feel free to mix quinoa and rice together for a textured blend. Black and red rice varieties add a more exotic feel to the dish. If you have problems digesting grains, use kelp noodle, quinoa, or millet.

recipe continues >>

Get Your Greens

- Dinosaur kale
- Curly kale
- Swiss chard
- Spinach

Get your greens on! If you are steaming (perfect for weight loss) or sautéing with a very small amount of coconut oil, double the quantity of greens you think you need as they will reduce considerably. Alternatively, skip cooking your greens altogether and instead lovingly massage some miso dressing into your raw kale.

Add More Whole Foods

- Yams
- Bananas
- Avocados

These should be virtually untouched. I simply bake the yam whole and cut it in half. Lightly sauté bananas sliced long in a very small amount of coconut oil. Avocado? Just slice a few wedges and add.

Probiotic Kraut

You can make your own kraut by following our recipe on page 109. Or you can try out the newest versions at your local farmers' market. Some varieties we enjoy are beet, ginger, spicy carrot, and traditional caraway seed.

Pick Your Sauces & Toppings

- Nut cheeses (pages 76–78)
- Tahini Green Sauce (page 95)
- Gluten-free tamari
- Fresh lemon juice
- Apple cider vinegar
- Large-grain Celtic sea salt
- Cinnamon
- Sesame seeds
- Pepitas
- Grated fresh ginger
- Grated fresh turmeric

VEGGIE BURGERS

It's been a journey experimenting with different versions of the coveted veggie burger and I can say that I've been down the veggie brick road a bit. Getting them to hold together through the cooking process and find their way onto the bun can be a bit of a challenge. However, I think I finally figured out a fail-proof way to outdo the classic burger in terms of taste, texture, and presentation. I prefer black beans but you can use adzuki as well. I've also found that short-grain brown rice made with a little extra water works best because it's so sticky. I keep the recipe very basic, which works well for my little girls who love to help me make them. Of course, feel free to add more veggies like diced green beans and carrots if you're inspired. Serve these burgers with sweet potato fries on a gluten-free bun, wrapped up inside a blanched collard green, or open face on a large, fresh, and crisp romaine leaf.

Ingredients

- 2 cups cooked dried black or adzuki beans
- 2 garlic cloves
- 8 cups filtered water
- 2 cups short-grain brown rice
- 1 small beet
- 1 teaspoon Celtic sea salt
- ¼ teaspoon fresh ground black pepper
- 2 tablespoons high-quality barbecue sauce
- 1 tablespoon ground flaxseeds
- 2 tablespoons arrowroot powder
- 1 tablespoon gluten-free tamari
- 1 teaspoon coconut oil, plus more for hands
- Fixings: lettuce, broccoli sprouts, fresh basil leaves, sliced tomato, fresh avocado, pickles (we like Bubbies brand), Vegenaise, ketchup, mustard, and Almond Pesto (page 102)

Preparation

1. Soak the dried beans overnight or bring to a boil, then turn off the heat and let sit for a few hours prior to cooking.

2. In a large pot, cook the beans and garlic in 3¾ cups filtered water over medium heat until soft but not mushy. This could take up to 2 hours. Drain.

3. In a large saucepan, mix the rice with 4¼ cups water and simmer over medium heat, covered, until the water is gone and the rice is moist. This will take approximately 30 minutes. Adding the extra ¼ cup water will produce a stickier rice. This helps the grains bind together more efficiently.

4. Simultaneously, in a small saucepan, boil the beet in water over high heat until done. This will take 30 to 40 minutes. Drain the water and rinse the beet in cold water.

recipe continues >>

5. Using your fingers, rub the skin off the beet. Then finely chop and set aside 2 tablespoons.

6. In a very large bowl, add the cooked rice and the drained cooked beans and allow them to cool for a few minutes.

7. After the mixture has cooled down, using your hands, start to mix the rice with the beans. Make an effort to squeeze the mixture through your fingers. This mashes the beans and starts to make the mixture bind. Get some help with this step. Little kids love this part!

8. Now add the diced beet, sea salt, pepper, barbecue sauce, flaxseeds, arrowroot, and tamari and mix again using your hands. If you did this correctly, you will have sticky fingers and the mixture will be hard to get off your hands. More fun for little chefs.

9. Rinse and dry your hands. Then apply a very small amount of coconut oil to your hands and start to form your burgers. When you have a patty size that is approximately the size of your bun, place it on a large plate. Continue until you've made 6 patties.

10. Cover the burgers with wax paper or a cloth and place in the refrigerator. I like to prepare the burgers ahead of time and let them stay in the fridge for at least 30 minutes for the flavors to combine and for the patties to firm up.

11. On a serving plate, arrange all the fixings.

12. In a cast-iron skillet, add the 1 teaspoon coconut oil and turn the flame on high. Sear the patties until brown on one side, then turn and heat through.

13. Transfer the burgers from the skillet directly onto the buns, then add the fixings. Lines of hungry children will appear, ready to plate up their burger. Devour!

GLUTEN-FREE STUFFING

Stuffing is a celebrated guest on our plates around the holidays. I cherish family tradition and heritage, so I promised my family that I would create a gluten-free, entirely plant-based, and all-around healthier version of stuffing that would satisfy their cravings and save a turkey in the process. This dish has lively and aromatic notes with fresh herbs, crisp celery, seaweed, and hearty mushrooms. It's an earthy stuffing with textures of the forest and a hint of the sea, buttressed by plenty of antioxidants. Switch up your normal stuffing and give this one a try. I promise it will delight!

Ingredients

- 2 loaves gluten-free bread
- ½ shallot, finely chopped
- 2 garlic cloves, peeled and finely chopped
- 1 tablespoon macadamia nut oil or olive oil
- 4 celery stalks, with leaves, chopped
- 2 cups wild mushrooms, washed and stems removed
- ½ small lemon
- 1 tablespoon gluten-free tamari
- 1 tablespoon chopped fresh sage
- 1 tablespoon chopped fresh thyme
- ¼ cup premium Atlantic organic seaweed, finely chopped
- 1 teaspoon large-grain Celtic sea salt (optional)
- 1 cup filtered water

Preparation

1. Preheat the oven to 350°F.

2. Cut the gluten-free bread loaves into ½" cubes. Spread them out evenly in a flat rectangular baking dish. Set aside.

3. In a large saucepan, sauté the shallot and garlic in the oil over medium heat for 30 seconds, then add the chopped celery and stir until the color brightens.

4. Add the mushrooms and continue to sauté until brown and the juices have made a nice broth in the pan.

5. Squeeze in the lemon and add the tamari and stir again.

6. Turn the sautéed mixture out over the bread cubes. Sprinkle with the fresh herbs and seaweed and mix well. If needed, add the sea salt.

7. Transfer to a large flat casserole dish. Add ½ cup of the filtered water. Cover the dish with aluminum foil or lid and bake for 30 minutes, until moist and heated through. Add the remaining ½ cup water, if needed.

Chef's Note: Be mindful that using store-bought gluten-free breads doesn't necessarily add up to healthy. You have to read the labels. If you can find a freshly baked millet bread at your farmers' market or at your local health food store, you'll be taking your game to the next level.

VEGGIE STIR-FRY

This is such a great easy dish that satisfies the entire family. The trick is to make it with almost no oil so that it tastes bright and fresh. Coconut oil is your best bet when it comes to cooking with oil as it holds up well at high heat. We use my old wok from my college days. It's missing the handle but it still delivers.

6

Ingredients

- 2 cups Thai purple sticky rice or brown rice
- 4¾ cups filtered water
- 1 head broccoli
- 4 carrots
- 1 head cauliflower
- 1 tablespoon coconut oil
- 1 cup snow peas
- 1 cup diced pineapple
- 1 cup raw cashews
- 1 cup sunflower sprouts or any variety sprouts
- Gluten-free tamari
- Juice of 1 lemon

Preparation

1. In a large saucepan, bring the rice and 4¼ cups water to a boil, then reduce the heat and cover. Simmer on medium to low heat until the water is absorbed and the rice is soft and moist, about 20 minutes.

2. Chop the broccoli, carrots, and cauliflower into bite-size pieces.

3. Heat a large wok over high heat and add the coconut oil. With the exception of the snow peas, add the veggies to the wok one at a time and allow the colors to brighten before adding the next veggie variety.

4. After about 4 minutes, add the remaining ½ cup water and cover. Let the veggies steam for a few minutes. Then add the snow peas and pineapple and steam until they are heated through. This entire process shouldn't take more than 8 minutes. You want your veggies crisp and bright. Don't overcook.

5. On a serving platter, arrange the rice mounded like a moat or thick ring around the outside.

6. Spoon the veggies into the center and garnish with cashews and fresh sprouts. Drizzle with gluten-free tamari and fresh lemon juice.

KIDS' MAC & CASHEW CHEESE

This dairy-free comfort dish seems to be an all-around favorite for the little kids in our lives, but it will put a serious smile on big kids' faces, too. The butternut squash, nutritional yeast, and cashews make it extra cheesy. With immune-boosting beta-carotene, the butternut squash keeps it healthy. We feel this dish is always best served with a very large plate of steaming broccoli.

Ingredients

CHEESY SAUCE

- ½ cup cooked butternut squash
- ½ cup raw cashews
- 2 tablespoons nutritional yeast
- 1 cup filtered water
- Squeeze of lemon
- ½ teaspoon Celtic sea salt
- Rice pasta or pasta of your choice

Preparation

1. Preheat the oven to 350°F.

2. Halve the butternut squash lengthwise and remove the seeds.

3. Place the squash skin-side down on a baking sheet and bake for 40 to 45 minutes, until soft and tender.

4. Scoop out the squash flesh. Set aside.

5. In a Vitamix or food processor, pulse the cashews until they are mealy in texture. Add the nutritional yeast and pulse again.

6. Add the butternut squash and water. Blend.

7. Finally, give a squeeze of lemon and add a bit of sea salt to taste.

8. Blend once more and there you have it! Yummy cheese sauce.

9. If you want it hotter, transfer it to a saucepan to heat and adjust the seasonings, or just keep that Vitamix running for a couple minutes.

10. Serve over rice pasta or pasta of your choice.

PORTABELLA PARMESANA

The almighty mushroom takes center stage in our Italian Portabella Parmesana. Mushrooms have a very high fiber and water content, which makes them a great option if you are trying to lose weight. They are also an excellent source of potassium, which helps the body process sodium and lower blood pressure. You can leave out the Almond Pesto (page 102) if you are on the Transformation path. Serve the mushrooms with a classic Caesar salad using our Caesar Salad Dressing (page 111) and enjoy a little taste of Italy.

Ingredients

- 6 large portobello mushrooms
- 6 tablespoons balsamic vinegar
- Blackened Tomato Cashew Sauce (page 101)
- Almond Pesto (page 102)
- Crumbled Walnut Parmesan (page 78)
- 1 cup fresh local sprouts

Preparation

1. Preheat the oven to 350°F.

2. Wash and stem the portobello mushrooms. Place them cap-side down, gills facing up, in a deep baking dish.

3. Add water until there is ¼" at the bottom of the dish. Make sure the water covers the bottom of the pan but does not spill over the mushrooms. Pour 1 tablespoon of balsamic vinegar into the center of each mushroom. Bake for 12 to 15 minutes or until they are juicy.

4. Transfer the mushrooms to a large, deep saucepan, cap-side down. Spoon a tablespoon of Almond Pesto in the center of each mushroom. Pour the tomato sauce over the mushrooms and simmer on low heat until the flavors are blended.

5. Sprinkle the Crumbled Walnut Parmesan over the tops of the mushrooms, garnish with sprouts, and serve.

TORRE DE NACHOS

Everyone in our family is always in the mood for this dish. It contains three of our all-time favorite recipes—Lemon Guacamole, Ginger Heirloom Salsa, and Cashew Cheese—which make it extra tasty. The flavors excite and it completely lives up to its Mexican heritage. While the beans are cooking, you can prepare the other ingredients, and assembly only takes a few minutes. A homerun every time.

Ingredients

- 2 cups dried or 2 (15-ounce) cans black beans, drained and rinsed
- About 6 cups filtered water
- 2 garlic cloves
- 1 teaspoon coconut oil
- Pinch asafetida
- 2 tablespoons ground cumin
- 2 teaspoons Celtic sea salt
- 2 big bags organic corn chips
- Lemon Guacamole (page 107)
- Ginger Heirloom Salsa (page 105)
- Cashew Cheese (page 76)
- Fresh cilantro, for garnish

Preparation

DRIED BLACK BEANS

Of course you can use canned black beans if you are short on time. If you go for making dried beans, you can double the quantity and store the excess in the fridge to use later in Veggie Burgers (page 199), or for a One Bowl (page 197). The energy of the food is better when you use dried black beans—and even higher-vibrating with sprouted black beans.

1. Soak the beans overnight in fresh water, or boil over high heat, turn off the heat, and set aside for a few hours.

2. In a large pot, add the beans, 6 cups filtered water, and the garlic.

Boil the beans over high heat until done. Add more water if needed and continue cooking to bring the beans to a soft consistency. Cooking dried beans will take up to 2 hours or more, depending on the soaking time and heat.

3. In a cast-iron skillet, heat the coconut oil over high. Add the asafetida and stir to temper for about 30 seconds.

4. Add cumin and sea salt to taste. Heat through.

recipe continues >>

Sprouted Black Beans

Sprouting black beans is pretty easy and should take 3 to 4 days. Give it a try.

1. Put a cup of beans in a colander and rinse really well. Cover them with a clean flour-sack cloth and set on the counter. Whenever you pass by them, give them a rinse. You will start to see the tails of the sprouts in 2 days. They will be done in 3 or 4 days, depending on the temperature of the room, the amount of rinsing, and the beans you used.

2. After they have sprouted, store them in the fridge in a sealed bag or mason jar. Always smell your sprouts and throw out anything that smells musty or moldy.

Nacho Assembly

Now we are ready to build this tasty nacho mountain. My family usually gathers around like we are at the starting line of some race. Hands are grabbing before I am even finished. They know these nachos won't last long.

1. On a large serving plate, arrange the chips in a deep layer, covering the entire surface.

2. Using a slotted spoon, place the beans on top of the chips, forming a layer covering as much area as possible while still leaving some chips visible.

3. Scoop the Lemon Guacamole in the center of the dish, forming a raised mound. Spoon the Ginger Heirloom Salsa on top of the guacamole and garnish with fresh cilantro.

4. Pour the Cashew Cheese sauce evenly over the previous layers. Garnish with fresh chopped cilantro and serve!

POTATO-QUINOA WRAPS WITH BRAZIL NUT CREAM

Warm, hearty potatoes and quinoa wrapped up in a large collard green makes a filling and fun lunch or dinner. The Brazil nut cream provides a wonderfully rich filling with copious healthy fats and vitamin E. The collard green gives you fiber plus vitamin C and is an excellent source of calcium, keeping your bones strong. Let everyone wrap their own. Serve these with our Cleansing Beet Soup (page 161). Enjoy!

Ingredients

- 3 pounds golden potatoes
- 2 tablespoons olive oil
- 1 teaspoon Celtic sea salt
- 2 cups red, yellow, or tricolor quinoa
- Brazil Nut Tomatillo Cream (page 103)
- 6 cups filtered water
- 6 collard green leaves
- 2 cups fresh sunflower sprouts
- Fermented Probiotic Kraut (page 109) or farmers' market variety kraut

Preparation

1. Preheat the oven to 375°F.

2. Dice the potatoes, leaving the skins on. Arrange in one layer on a baking tray. Drizzle with the olive oil and sprinkle with the salt. Roast until tender and slightly crispy. This should take approximately 30 minutes.

3. In a medium saucepan, bring 4 cups water to a boil. Add the quinoa, reduce the heat to medium, and cover. Simmer until the liquid is absorbed and the quinoa opens.

4. When the potatoes are ready, transfer them to a large saucepan and fold in the nut cream.

5. Bring the filtered water to a boil in a medium pan. Quickly blanch each collard green leaf one at a time. Using tongs, hold each leaf in the boiling water until the color brightens. This will take about 1 minute for each leaf. Remove and set on a paper towel. Pat dry (blanching will tenderize the leaves and make them easy to bite into).

6. Run a knife down the center vein of the blanched collard green. This will make it easier to fold the leaves.

7. On a serving plate, lay one blanched collard green flat. Spoon the quinoa onto the middle and add the potato-nut cream mixture. Garnish with sunflower sprouts and kraut. Wrap the bottoms up and fold in the sides to form a pouch.

TAMALES DE REGALOS

Small packages of delight, these tamales are succulent gifts around the holidays or the perfect treat to add to any Mexican-inspired meal. The trick is making them small and delicate so they melt in your mouth instead of feeling like a load in your belly. Gather the whole family around and enjoy the conversation and comedy as you learn to wrap them. Serve these with extra Tomatillo Salsa (page 104), Fast Raw Mole (page 100), or Lemon Guacamole (page 107).

Ingredients

- 8 ears organic corn with husks
- 4 cups organic masa or cornmeal
- 1 teaspoon Celtic sea salt
- 1 tablespoon baking powder
- 1 cup Earth Balance vegan butter, at room temperature
- 1 cup filtered water
- ¼ cup Brazil Nut Tomatillo Cream (page 103)
- ¼ cup cinnamon

FILLING

- 10 basil leaves
- 6 sun-dried tomatoes
- 1 cup raw pepitas
- 1 cup dried cranberries

Preparation

1. Strip the corn husks from the cobs; remove the silky strings and discard into your compost bin. Place the green husks in a large bowl of water to soak. Reserve the cobs to roast over a fire later.

2. To a large bowl, add the masa, salt, and baking powder; mix well with a wooden spoon. Add the softened vegan butter and mix it into the dry masa with your hands. Keep working the butter until it is well incorporated. Add the water in ¼-cup increments until the dough holds together like a drop cookie dough.

3. Divide the dough in half and place in two separate bowls. Add the tomatillo cream to one half and the cinnamon to the other. Mix well with your hands.

4. Finely chop the basil and sun-dried tomatoes. Set aside.

5. On a flat surface, lay a green corn husk flat and spread 2 tablespoons of the masa mixture into the center of the husk.

6. For the cinnamon version, sprinkle some pepitas and dried cranberries into the center of the masa. For the tomatillo version, spoon a teaspoon of the chopped sun-dried tomatoes and basil into the center of the masa. Carefully fold in the sides of the corn husk, fold up the bottom, and fold down the top to wrap your package of tamale. Tie off with a thin long string of corn husk.

7. Steam on high heat for 25 minutes in a steamer pot.

ROASTED TOMATO CACAO SAUCE OVER PENNE

Ripe cherry tomatoes, nuts, and cacao all blended into one creamy sauce take regular pasta sauce to a whole new level. This recipe is an antioxidant powerhouse of flavors. Lycopene may reduce your risk of heart disease, improve vision, and lower bad cholesterol. Super-nutritious cacao nibs add a real depth of flavor. Pair with our Warm Mushroom Salad (page 169) and dinner is served.

Ingredients

- 1 cup organic cherry tomatoes
- 6 large basil leaves
- 3 dehydrated sun-dried tomatoes
- 2 Brazil nuts
- 2 tablespoons pine nuts
- 1 tablespoon cacao nibs
- 2 tablespoons olive oil
- ½ teaspoon Celtic sea salt
- ⅛ teaspoon fresh ground black pepper
- Gluten-free penne or other pasta
- 2 cups organic cherry tomatoes, halved, for garnish
- ¼ cup pine nuts, for garnish
- 1 sprig fresh thyme, for garnish

Preparation

1. In a wok or cast-iron skillet over high heat, no oil, slightly blacken the cherry tomatoes. If the pan is hot, this should take no more than 5 minutes.

2. To a blender or Vitamix, add the cherry tomatoes and all the other ingredients; blend on high for a full minute.

3. Pour over gluten-free penne or your favorite pasta.

4. Garnish with cherry tomatoes, pine nuts, and thyme.

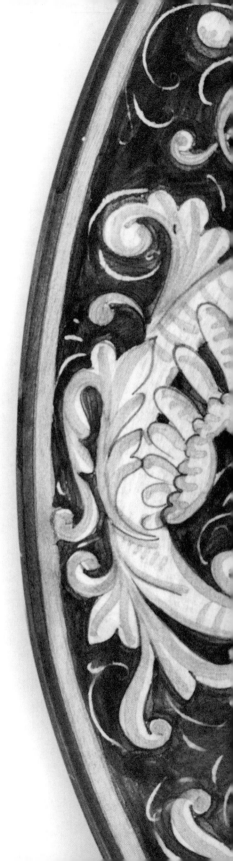

AZTEC ENCHILADAS

Enchiladas are my all-time favorite Mexican dish. So I had to dig deep to come up with a healthier dairy-free version that stayed true to its roots while still satisfying my cravings. Predictably, my creativity went wild, taking me deep inside the central regions of Mexico. Chia seeds, the energy source of the great Aztec runners, add a superfood boost in this recipe. Teeming with vitality, our Fast Raw Mole blankets this dish in flavors that pay worthy tribute to Oaxaca. The rich earthiness of red potatoes with spinach, chia seeds, and olives smothered in raw mole sauce delivers savory ancient wisdom in each and every bite.

Ingredients

- 4 pounds red potatoes
- 3 tablespoons nutritional yeast, plus more for sprinkling
- 2 tablespoons miso paste
- Juice of 1 large lemon
- 2 tablespoons chia seeds
- ¼ cup filtered water
- 2 teaspoons plus a pinch of Celtic sea salt
- Fresh ground black pepper, to taste
- 2 bunches fresh spinach
- 1 tablespoon coconut oil or macadamia nut oil
- 1 tablespoon apple cider vinegar
- ½ cup chopped green olives
- ½ cup chopped black olives
- 12 small flour or corn tortillas
- Fast Raw Mole (page 100)
- ½ cup chopped fresh cilantro

Preparation

1. Preheat the oven to 350°F.

2. In a large pot, boil the potatoes in water until tender. This takes approximately 30 minutes over very high heat. You'll know they are done when a fork slides effortlessly into the center.

3. Remove the skins with your fingers while simultaneously rinsing the potatoes under cold water. The cold water will protect your fingers from the hot potato! The skins should slide right off.

4. Cut the potatoes into bite-size pieces and transfer to a medium bowl. Set aside.

5. In a small bowl, using a wire whisk, mix the nutritional yeast, miso paste, lemon juice, chia seeds, and filtered water until well combined. Pour this mixture over the potatoes and combine well, turning the mixture over and over with your hands. Add 2 teaspoons of the sea salt and pepper to taste. Mix again and adjust the seasonings.

recipe continues >>

6. In a wok or cast-iron skillet, sauté the spinach over medium heat in the coconut oil. The spinach will drastically reduce. Sauté only until it starts to wilt—don't kill it.

7. Remove from the heat, add the apple cider vinegar and the pinch of sea salt. Turn the spinach to incorporate the vinegar and salt.

8. Add the spinach and chopped olives to the potato mixture and stir to combine.

9. Spoon approximately 2 tablespoons of the potato mixture into a tortilla and wrap.

10. Set the tortillas in a rectangular baking dish, placing the folded side down. Cover and smother in our Fast Raw Mole, making sure to coat the edges of the tortillas. Cover with aluminum foil and bake for 25 minutes, until heated through.

11. Remove the foil. Sprinkle with nutritional yeast and garnish with chopped cilantro.

Devour!

Chef's Note: I also happen to adore these enchiladas with my green Tomatillo Salsa (page 104).

PORTOBELLO MUSHROOM BURGERS

Mushroom burger night: this vegan alternative to the classic burger is always a winner. Biting into this pile of deliciousness makes for a perfect and easy weeknight meal. If you don't have time to make my Veggie Burgers (page 199), try this much simpler recipe. Large superfood portobello mushrooms provide not only hearty flavor and texture but plenty of real food nutrition, and with all the fixings, the burgers will leave you feeling deeply satisfied. This is a superior option to a store-bought frozen veggie burger! You'll be eating whole foods!

Ingredients

- 6 medium to large portobello mushrooms
- 6 tablespoons balsamic vinegar
- Burger buns
- Vegenaise
- Broccoli sprouts
- Sliced tomato
- Ketchup
- Yellow mustard
- Bubbies dill pickles

Preparation

1. Preheat the oven to 350°F.

2. Wash and stem the mushrooms. In a shallow baking dish, arrange the portobello mushrooms cap-side down, with the gills facing up.

3. Pour ¼ cup water into the bottom of the baking dish. This will keep the mushrooms from getting dry.

4. Measure 1 tablespoon of the balsamic vinegar into the center of each mushroom cap. Tip the mushrooms from side to side and all around so that the vinegar seeps into the gills on the mushroom.

5. Bake for 10 to 12 minutes, or until the juices release.

6. Build your burger.

7. Warm the buns in the oven while it's still hot. On one side, spread Vegenaise; add the sprouts and tomato. On the opposite side, spread ketchup and mustard and top with a mushroom cap. Put the sides together and take a juicy bite.

8. Bubbies dill pickles on the side give you all the amino acids you need to digest your food. You can find these at Whole Foods or any health food market.

SUPERFOOD PAD THAI

Almost entirely raw, this fresh peanut and hemp seed pad Thai is quick to prepare and fabulously satisfies any Thai food craving. Feed your body temple a golden offering that's packed with superfoods and fit for a Buddha! Hydrating cucumbers help flush out your kidneys and reduce inflammation while the probiotic sauerkraut aids digestion and keeps the immune system strong. Your body will worship this homemade Thai food delight!

Ingredients

- 1 large cucumber
- 3 tablespoons apple cider vinegar
- 1 squeeze lemon juice
- Splash namah shoyu
- 1 (8-ounce) package rice pad Thai noodles
- Small bunch basil
- Small bunch cilantro
- Raw Peanut Sauce (page 108)
- ½ cup fermented veggies or probiotic sauerkraut
- 2 tablespoons hemp seeds

Preparation

1. Peel and dice the cucumber. Place the pieces in a medium bowl with the apple cider vinegar, lemon juice, and namah shoyu. Toss and set aside.

2. Cook the noodles according to the package directions; drain and rinse well.

3. Loosely chop the basil and cilantro, leaving a few leaves whole for garnish.

4. On a large serving platter, arrange the noodles in a thin layer to cover the plate.

5. Pour the fresh Raw Peanut Sauce over the noodles.

6. Add the cucumber mixture, topped with the fermented veggies or sauerkraut.

7. Garnish with hemp seeds, basil, and cilantro. Serve!

GLUTEN-FREE SPAGHETTI DI PESTO

When it comes to gluten-free pasta, I like a spaghetti brown rice version because it's thin, delicate, and holds its own when seasoned with a great sauce. The Almond Pesto in this recipe is so delicious, and it makes all varieties of veggies taste even more amazing. Enjoy this beautiful pasta dish for lunch, dinner, brunch, or a late-night snack.

Ingredients

- 1 package gluten-free brown rice spaghetti
- 1 red bell pepper
- ½ cup raw pumpkin seeds
- 1 cup Almond Pesto (page 102)
- 1 cup broccoli or any variety of fresh sprouts
- 3 basil leaves
- 1 teaspoon olive oil
- Cracked black pepper to taste
- ½ teaspoon Celtic sea salt

Preparation

1. Bring a large pot of water to a boil and prepare the spaghetti according to the package directions.

2. Dice the bell pepper in ⅛" pieces, discarding the stem and seeds.

3. On a flat tray or cookie sheet, toast the pumpkin seeds at 350°F for about 8 minutes, or until slightly golden brown.

4. When the spaghetti is done, rinse well with hot water and turn out into a large pasta bowl. Add the pesto and stir well to evenly distribute throughout the spaghetti. Add the diced bell peppers, roasted pumpkin seeds, and broccoli or fresh sprouts. Garnish with basil leaves and a drizzle of olive oil. Season with fresh cracked pepper and sea salt.

KELP NOODLES & PURPLE KALE

This dish would make an awesome name for a psychedelic '60s band. A pure vitamin K high, it would make Paul McCartney smile. Purple kale really makes this dish pop with color and the fiber and vitamin K it contains work with calcium to support the processes necessary to build strong bones. Kelp noodles are a great substitute for wheat or flour pasta noodles. They contain iodine, which plays a key role in metabolism and thyroid function. This is a fabulous one-dish meal full of delicious flavors and colors.

Ingredients

- 12 ounces kelp noodles
- 2 cups filtered water
- 1 cup purple Thai sticky rice
- 2 bunches purple kale or any kale variety
- Asian Dressing (page 115)
- 1 large red bell pepper
- 1 bunch fresh mint, for garnish
- 2 tablespoons tamari
- 1 tablespoon coconut oil
- 31 ounces sprouted tofu, cubed
- Peanut sauce or teriyaki sauce, for serving

Preparation

1. Bring a large pot of water to a boil on high for the kelp noodles.

2. In a medium saucepan, bring the filtered water and Thai rice to a boil, then reduce the heat, cover, and simmer until the water is absorbed and the rice is tender, about 30 minutes.

3. While the rice is cooking, stem the kale leaves by holding the leaves and stripping them from the center stalk. Tear the kale into 3" pieces.

4. In a medium bowl, toss the kale leaves with the Asian Dressing.

5. Using your hands, massage the dressing into the kale leaves, until the they begin to soften. Set aside.

6. Dice the bell pepper and chop the mint; set aside.

7. Boil the kelp noodles in the boiling water for 2 minutes. Drain.

8. In a large wok, heat the coconut oil. Grill the tofu on high heat until slightly browned, pour the tamari over the tofu, turn and repeat on the other side.

9. On individual serving plates, prepare a bed of kale, then add the kelp noodles, sticky rice, and grilled tofu. Drizzle with a good-quality peanut sauce or teriyaki sauce. (If you want to use a homemade sauce, try our Raw Peanut Sauce, page 108.)

10. Garnish with the red bell pepper and mint.

CAULIFLOWER GOLDEN BEET TACOS

This is a gourmet variation of classic tacos. We enjoyed a version of these tasty delights at Tia Belinda's house during a recent *Game of Thrones* marathon. Belinda is a great cook from a Mexican family with roots in the local area. I adore spending time in her kitchen as she always has something amazing brewing. These tacos are filled with golden beets and blackened cauliflower. Belinda sautés them up a bit on the spicy side, which gives a lively kick to the beautiful earthy flavors of the veggies. This taco creation is sure to put your family on a healthier path.

Ingredients

- 1 bunch golden beets, with greens
- 2 tablespoons grape seed oil
- 2 tablespoons balsamic vinegar
- Celtic sea salt, to taste
- 1 head cauliflower
- 2 small green onions, diced

- 3 tablespoons olive oil, plus more to taste
- 1 teaspoon chili powder
- ½ jalapeño, diced (optional)
- 8 small corn tortillas
- 1 cup Kalamata or gourmet olives, sliced, for serving
- Brazil Nut Tomatillo Cream (page 103)
- Tomatillo Salsa (page 104)

DRESSING

- 1 tablespoon apple cider vinegar
- 1 teaspoon grape seed oil
- ¼ teaspoon Celtic sea salt
- 1 head iceberg lettuce, cut into long strips
- 1 bunch cilantro, stems removed

Preparation

1. Wash the beets well. Remove the greens and cut off the roots and stems. Dice the beets into small, ¼" pieces. Chop the beet greens into small, bite-size pieces and set aside.

2. Sauté the beets over medium heat in a large saucepan in the grape seed oil. After they begin to brown, add a bit of water to the pan and simmer until soft.

3. Transfer the beets to a serving bowl. Drizzle with the balsamic vinegar and sprinkle with salt to taste. Set aside.

4. Remove the base and leaves from the cauliflower and marvel at the way it looks like a miniature tree. Slice the heads and branches in small, bite-size pieces. Discard the thicker stems and base.

5. Sauté the white tops of the green onions in 2 tablespoons of the olive oil until soft. Add the cauliflower and sauté until it begins to brown.

6. Sprinkle the cauliflower and onion sauté with the chili powder and add the jalapeño if you like the kick.

7. Add ¼ cup water to the pan and simmer until the cauliflower is soft. Transfer to a serving bowl, drizzle with olive oil, and sprinkle with salt to taste.

8. In the same pan, sauté the beet greens in 1 tablespoon of the olive oil until wilted. Drizzle with namah shoyu or gluten-free tamari. Transfer to the serving bowl.

9. In the bottom of a salad bowl, prepare the dressing by whisking together the apple cider vinegar, grape seed oil, and sea salt. Add the iceberg lettuce and ½ cup cilantro leaves. Toss.

10. Place a tortilla over an open flame on a gas stove or place in a dry cast-iron skillet. Using a set of tongs, turn the tortilla after 10 seconds or so. Repeat on the opposite side, until the tortilla is soft. Transfer to a serving plate.

11. Serve with olives, our Brazil Nut Tomatillo Cream, and Tomatillo Salsa. Garnish with cilantro and green onion.

12. Arrange all the serving bowls buffet-style. Let your family build their own perfect taco.

MASHED POTATOES

When we started on our plant-based journey, this was a dish that fulfilled our need for real comfort food. These steamy pillows of red potatoes also helped Rich's athletic performance, giving him the necessary carbs to replenish his body from a hard day of training and boosting his energy for the following day. Leaving the skins on not only looks great but also provides additional nutrients. Filled with vitamins C and B$_6$ and fiber, this warm dish is simply divine. Here's a great way to get your "mashed" on.

Ingredients

- 5 pounds red potatoes
- ¼ cup olive oil
- ½ cup Vegenaise
- 2 teaspoons large-grain Celtic sea salt
- Fresh ground black pepper, to taste

Preparation

1. In a large pot, boil the potatoes in water until a fork inserted slides in easily. Drain the potatoes and return to the pot.

2. With the heat on low, add the olive oil and start to cut the potatoes crosswise repeatedly until all the potatoes are cut in small sections.

3. Turn off the heat and add the Vegenaise, salt, and pepper to taste.

4. Using a large spoon, incorporate all the ingredients until you have the consistency of a country-style mashed potato dish. You will still have some chunks and pieces of the red skins visible within a creamy base.

CAULIFLOWER MASHED POTATOES

Cauliflower gets such a bad rap. You might be surprised to learn that this anti-inflammatory, heart-healthy flowering vegetable is incredibly nutritious, very versatile, and actually quite sweet. It may even help protect you against certain cancers and is packed with vitamins. If you are on the Transformation path, have health issues, or you just want to eat higher-quality, more nutritionally dense plants, then this is your kind of mashed. Still think you don't like cauliflower? Go ahead and try it! We dare you.

Ingredients

- 1 head cauliflower
- 5 pounds red potatoes
- ¼ cup chickpea, brown rice, or soy-based miso paste, plus more if needed
- ¼ cup nutritional yeast
- 1 teaspoon large-grain Celtic sea salt
- ⅛ teaspoon fresh ground black pepper

Preparation

1. In a large steamer pot, steam the cauliflower until it's tender, about 25 minutes. When it's ready, the color will become a bit translucent and a knife will easily loosen the florets. You want the cauliflower to be soft enough to mash, so don't understeam it, or you will have crunchy pieces in your mashed potatoes.

2. While the cauliflower is steaming, boil the potatoes in water until a fork inserted slides in easily. Drain the potatoes and return to the pot.

3. With the heat on low to draw any excess moisture out of potatoes, add the miso paste and start to cut the potatoes with a large knife crosswise repeatedly until all are cut in small sections.

4. Turn off the heat and add the steamed cauliflower.

5. Keep cutting crosswise in all directions until the cauliflower is well incorporated with the potatoes. Fold in the nutritional yeast, salt, and pepper.

6. Mix well and adjust for seasoning, adding more miso paste, if needed.

FETTUCCINI ALFREDO

I'm certain the original "Alfredo" would approve of this warm and satisfying "cheese" sauce. This dish that screams "comfort food!" is simply butternut squash blended with nutritional yeast. The squash provides a nice beta-carotene boost with lots of vitamin C and B vitamins to keep you healthy and in a great mood. Hints of nutmeg and fresh sage provide an aromatic earthiness and flavor to this sauce.

Ingredients

- ½ cup cashews
- Filtered water
- 1 butternut squash
- 2 tablespoons nutritional yeast
- ¼ teaspoon Celtic sea salt
- 1 cup hot filtered water
- 2 tablespoons Earth Balance vegan butter
- ⅛ teaspoon fresh cracked black pepper
- ¼ teaspoon nutmeg, plus a sprinkle for garnish
- ½ teaspoon chopped sage, plus leaves for garnish
- 1 small garlic clove, peeled
- 1 package fettuccini (preferably rice or mung bean)
- 1 tablespoon walnut oil

Preparation

1. Preheat the oven to 400°F.

2. Soak the cashews in filtered water for a minimum of 4 hours or overnight.

3. Place the entire butternut squash on a wire rack in the middle of the oven. Bake until done, about 40 minutes. Remove the skin and halve lengthwise to scoop out the seeds.

4. In a Vitamix or high-powered blender, combine the drained soaked cashews, nutritional yeast, sea salt, hot water, about 2 cups of the roasted squash, and the vegan butter. If the consistency is too thick, add more water in ¼-cup increments.

5. Finally, add the pepper, nutmeg, sage, and garlic. Blend again and adjust the seasonings to taste.

6. Prepare the fettuccini according to the package directions. Drain the pasta in a colander and turn it out into a large serving bowl. Drizzle with the walnut oil and toss to coat.

7. On individual plates, arrange a mound of fettuccini noodles in the center. Pour the warm sauce over the fettuccini. Garnish with fresh sage leaves and sprinkle with more nutmeg, sea salt, and cracked pepper.

UNTUNA WRAPS

This is an amazingly easy, off-the-hook-tasty recipe. My sons say that the only thing missing from this tuna is the mercury—well put! I sometimes crave the tuna sandwich taste from my childhood memories. My little girls asked me recently, "Mom, what is a tuna sandwich?" Although they have been enjoying this walnut and olive–based recipe for years, it wasn't until that moment that I realized they had nothing to compare it to, as they have never actually eaten a real tuna sandwich! After collecting myself, I replied, "It's a fish." They protested, "Why would you eat a fish? That's an animal!" I had to stop to ask myself the same question: *Why would I?* Well, now you, too, can say so long to your classic tuna salad. It's actually uncanny how much this dish tastes like tuna—and that's a promise.

Ingredients

- 1½ cups raw walnuts
- 1 cup pitted Kalamata olives
- ¼ cup seaweed or sea veggies
- 2 celery stalks, coarsely chopped
- 2 tablespoons Bubbies relish with amino acids
- Romaine leaves, collard greens, or your favorite bread

Preparation

1. In a food processor, pulse the walnuts until mealy in texture.

2. Add the olives and sea veggies. Process again for 30 seconds or until well incorporated.

3. Turn the mixture out into a medium bowl and fold in the chopped celery and relish.

4. Spread on romaine leaves, wrap in a blanched collard green, or spread on your favorite bread. We love hemp bread and gluten-free millet varieties.

RISOTTO

In my opinion, risotto should be served either before or after the largest raw salad you can muster, and is best finished off with fresh fruit or sorbet. Risotto is very heavy and filling, so make sure you keep your portions *piccolo*, as they say in Italy. The key to creating great cheesy-tasting risotto is to use a combination of nutritional yeast and Crumbled Walnut Parmesan. I use fresh garlic in all these dishes to honor the hardworking Italian mothers who inspired me to continue the risotto tradition.

Raspberry

I used to produce yoga retreats, annually taking groups to a stunning *agriturismo* farmhouse in the Tuscany region of Italy. It was more than fifteen years ago, but I still vividly recall Rich and me savoring an otherworldly strawberry risotto in Sienna. *It was that good.* Here I present my own version with fresh raspberries, inspired by this unique traditional Northern Italian dish.

Ingredients

- 1 garlic clove, finely chopped
- 1 tablespoon olive oil
- 2 cups high-quality Arborio rice
- 8 to 10 cups filtered water
- 1 cup nutritional yeast
- 2 teaspoons Celtic sea salt, plus more to taste
- 1 bunch arugula
- 1 bunch basil
- 1 lemon
- ¼ cup raw walnuts
- 1 cup fresh raspberries
- 1 tablespoon high-quality balsamic glaze
- Crumbled Walnut Parmesan (page 78)

Preparation

1. In a large saucepan, sauté the garlic in the olive oil over medium heat.

2. Add the rice and stir to coat. Add 1 cup filtered water and stir until it absorbs, then add another cup. Continue to add water until the rice is soft, moist, and creamy. This usually takes 30 to 40 minutes.

3. Sprinkle the nutritional yeast and sea salt to taste over the rice. Stir until it is mixed in. Adjust the seasoning to taste. Set aside.

4. Chop the arugula and basil in ribbons about ⅛" wide.

5. In a small bowl, squeeze the lemon juice and sprinkle in the 2 teaspoons sea salt. Toss to coat.

6. Just before serving, fold in the arugula and basil along with the walnuts and fresh raspberries. Drizzle with the balsamic glaze. Sprinkle with Crumbled Walnut Parmesan.

Wild Mushroom

This superfood winter version
is warm and hearty. Mushrooms
provide more than just taste and
texture to a meal; they have a
high nutritional value. Packed
with nutrients like niacin, iron,
potassium, vitamin B_6, magnesium,
and selenium, they do a great job
of protecting your body against
disease. This is such a comforting
dish to add to your family favorites.
A great complement to a roaring fire,
good friends, and lots of laughs.

Ingredients

- 1 garlic clove, finely chopped
- 2 cups good-quality Arborio rice
- 2 tablespoons olive oil
- 8 to 10 cups filtered water
- 1 cup nutritional yeast
- 2 teaspoons Celtic sea salt
- 2 cups wild field mushrooms
- 1 lemon
- 1 tablespoon gluten-free tamari
- Small bunch wild sage
- Small bunch thyme
- Crumbled Walnut Parmesan
(page 78)

recipe continues >>

Preparation

1. Prepare the risotto as in steps 1 to 3 on page 230.

2. In a small cast-iron skillet or wok, sauté the mushrooms in 1 tablespoon olive oil until the juices release.

3. Squeeze the lemon juice over the top and add a dash of gluten-free tamari.

4. Chop the sage and thyme finely. Fold into the rice mixture and sprinkle with Crumbled Walnut Parmesan.

Lobster Mushroom

Lobster mushrooms are locally harvested here in California but available only once per year. They boast a beautiful, bright red-orange color and have a surprisingly sea-like taste. I discovered these gems by accident at our farmers' market and had to give them a spin. They look so much like their namesake that when I posted this dish on my Instagram I was accused of using real lobster!

Ingredients

- 2 cups high-quality Arborio rice
- 1 garlic clove, finely chopped
- 3 tablespoons olive oil
- 2 teaspoons Celtic sea salt
- 8 to 10 cups filtered water
- 1 cup nutritional yeast
- 2 cups lobster mushrooms, chopped
- 1 cup wood ear mushrooms, chopped
- 1 lemon
- 2 tablespoons raw seaweed
- Crumbled Walnut Parmesan (page 78)

Preparation

1. Prepare the risotto according to steps 1 to 3 on page 230.

2. In a cast-iron skillet or wok, sauté the lobster mushrooms in 2 tablespoons olive oil until the juices release.

3. Add the wood ear mushrooms and sauté for another minute. Squeeze the lemon over the mushrooms.

4. Fold the mushrooms into the rice until well distributed.

5. Cut the seaweed with scissors into fine strips, sprinkle over the rice, and fold in.

6. Top with Crumbled Walnut Parmesan.

AROMATIC COUNTRY-STYLE TEMPEH LOAF

A far cry from the traditional meat loaf that I loathed as a child, this meatless loaf is one of our family favorites. It's hearty, filling, and really hits the spot during the holidays and colder winter months. Tempeh has a neutral taste with rich textures. It provides an opportunity to present an array of lively flavors, so don't be shy with your seasonings! Serve it with one of our Mashed Potato versions (pages 224 and 225), Candied Ginger Island Cranberry Sauce (page 94), some sautéed Swiss chard, and of course our Simple Mushroom Gravy (page 97).

Ingredients

- 2 large tempeh slabs (13" x 5", or 4 pounds)
- Filtered water
- 1 (8-ounce) bottle high-quality barbecue sauce or teriyaki-style marinade
- ½ beet
- 1 large carrot
- 1 medium zucchini
- 1 cup lake green beans
- 2 shallots, sliced
- 1 tablespoon olive oil
- 1 tablespoon fresh oregano
- 1 tablespoon fresh thyme
- 1 tablespoon fresh rosemary
- 2 tablespoons ground cumin
- 2 tablespoons arrowroot powder
- 2 teaspoons Celtic sea salt
- Blackened Tomato Cashew Sauce (page 101)

Preparation

1. Preheat the oven to 350°F.

2. Soak the tempeh slabs in filtered water for at least 30 minutes. Drain.

3. Crumble the tempeh into a large bowl.

4. Add the entire bottle of barbecue sauce to the tempeh mixture and mix well. Set aside for at least 2 hours.

5. Boil the beet in water until soft (about 30 minutes), peel, and chop. Chop and dice all the other veggies and mix in. Set aside.

6. Brown the sliced shallots in the olive oil and add to the tempeh.

7. Finally add the oregano, thyme, rosemary, cumin, arrowroot, and sea salt. Using your hands, mix it all up and start to form a loaf shape in the center of a large rectangular baking dish. You can also use a loaf pan.

8. Pour the Blackened Tomato Cashew Sauce over the top; cover and bake until heater through, about 40 minutes.

9. There you have it. A meat loaf you can fall in love with.

6

COCONUT CURRY

There is nothing quite like a great hearty curry when you're craving the exotic on your dinner table. I like to serve a steaming coconut version over a mixture of jasmine rice and heirloom black rice. Using an abundance of fresh herbs produces a pungent aromatic flavor that complements its milky smooth texture. You can up the kick in your curry by adding more jalapeño. Invest in a high-quality curry powder—it makes a difference!

Ingredients

- 2 cups white jasmine rice
- 1 cup black heirloom rice
- 1 sweet Maui onion
- 2 large garlic cloves
- 2 cups carrot
- ½ jalapeño
- 1 tablespoon coconut oil
- 4 cups diced broccoli florets
- 4 cups cauliflower florets
- 2 cups diced zucchini
- 6 tablespoons curry powder
- 2 tablespoons grated fresh ginger
- Juice of 3 limes
- 6 cups filtered water
- 2 cups grated fresh coconut
- 1 cup fresh basil
- 1 cup fresh cilantro
- ⅓ cup lemongrass (optional)
- 1 (15-ounce) can coconut cream
- 2 teaspoons Celtic sea salt

Preparation

1. Steam the rice according to the package directions.

2. Finely slice the onions in delicate rings and cut into quarters.

3. Slice the ends off the garlic cloves and mash them with the flat side of a large knife. Remove the center green sprout. Finely chop and set aside.

4. Slice the carrots into thin rounds. Slice the jalapeño into thin rounds then quarter them, removing any seeds. Set aside.

In a large saucepan, heat the coconut oil over medium heat. Add the onion and sauté until slightly brown. Now add the carrots, broccoli, and cauliflower, sautéing for 1 minute between each veggie. Now, add the zucchini and sauté, stirring continuously. The zucchini should release some water, which will prepare the veggies to receive the spices in the next step.

5. Add the curry powder, chopped garlic, ginger, jalapeño, and lime juice. Stir to coat the veggies well.

6. Now pour in the water and add the fresh coconut. Put a lid on the pot and allow the curry to come to a medium boil.

7. Chop the basil, cilantro, and lemongrass (if using) into small pieces, reserving some whole leaves for garnish.

8. Turn off the heat. Add the coconut cream and stir well with a wooden spoon. Sprinkle in the Celtic sea salt. Adjust the seasonings to taste.

9. Serve the curry poured over freshly steamed rice.

10. Garnish with basil, fresh cilantro, and lemongrass.

Chef's Note: Grate fresh coconut on a box grater or use coconut flakes (found in the bulk section of health food markets).

VEGAN LASAGNA

Dubbed "the best vegan lasagna ever!" by wellness pioneer and MindBodyGreen.com founder, Jason Wachob, this crowd-pleaser is rich in zesty flavor, delightfully cheesy, and certain to win over even a hardened carnivore. We recently prepared it for eighty hungry guests at a friend's wedding reception. Instead of being intimidated by the prospect of serving so many, we turned it into a fun family project that entailed borrowing extra lasagna pans from around the neighborhood while the kids formed a well-oiled assembly line of washers, slicers, choppers, and bakers. It was a hit! Slicing the zucchinis thin can be tricky, even with a sharp knife. To take your game to the next level, get yourself a mandoline like the one shown in our Equipment List (page 32). It will save you so much time and effort in attaining super-thin slices. However, be extremely careful with the blade. We use protective gloves religiously, preferring to save our fingers for playing the guitar.

Ingredients

- 16 large zucchinis
- Olive oil, for greasing
- Almond Pesto (page 102)
- Blackened Tomato Cashew Sauce (page 101)
- Crumbled Walnut Parmesan (page 78)
- 3 whole basil leaves, for garnish

recipe continues >>

Preparation

1. Preheat the oven to 350°F.

2. While wearing protective gloves, use a mandoline to slice the zucchinis lengthwise into ⅛"-thick sections to present wide, flat lasagna noodles. I try to select the largest zucchinis and buy more than I need. This allows me to find the widest noodle pieces from the largest sections of zucchini. You can save the extra noodles and use them later in our Grilled Veggie Salad (page 172).

3. In a large deep rectangular lasagna dish, lightly oil the bottom and sides with olive oil using a paper towel.

4. Arrange two layers of zucchini in a basketweave pattern across the bottom of the dish.

5. Using a spoon and your fingers, spread 1 teaspoon of the Almond Pesto across each zucchini noodle.

6. Add another layer of the zucchini in a basketweave pattern and spread the pesto on each noodle. Repeat until you have arrived at the end of your zucchini and reached the upper portion of the dish.

7. Pour 3 cups of the Blackened Tomato Cashew Sauce over the zucchini and make sure that the sauce spreads over the entire surface.

8. Cover with aluminum foil and bake for 30 to 40 minutes, or until the zucchini is soft when a fork is inserted into it. Remove from the oven and remove the foil.

9. Sprinkle a layer of Crumbled Walnut Parmesan over the top and garnish with fresh basil leaves.

EMBRACING THE NOW

What if you knew that you were already perfect exactly where you are, *right now*, in this moment? Our minds are mischievously clever. Time and again, they pull us back to the past and yank us forward into the future. Our perception of the world—and the story we tell ourselves about who we are—is completely colored by half-baked memories and imagined projections. But in truth this is all illusion, fabricated by the errant meanderings of our wayward-thinking minds. The only objective truth is the present moment—*the now*.

Everything you have ever done, thought, seen, and felt in your life has led you to this exact point in time where you are now holding this book in your hands, reading these words. There is no accident in this indisputable reality.

We say embrace it all! From the heroic triumphs to the colossal failures and everything in between, the experiences of your life compose the story you tell yourself about who you are. But that identity is merely a composite of self-imposed value judgments about an infinitesimal cross section of the infinite moments that actually comprise your life. In other words, the events we focus on to form this "story" are not good, bad, happy, or sad until we *decide* to so categorize them.

Understanding that you have the power to liberate yourself from that story and frame a new narrative is the path toward unlocking your true authentic self, and ultimately freedom.

To understand these principles is to embrace the idea that there is no place for regret, resentment, guilt, shame, or self-flogging. *It's OK.* Really. All of it. So breathe. Let it go. And trust that all will be well. The Universe is all knowing, and it has a plan for you. That's a promise.

Whether you've come to this Plantpower lifestyle through a deep desire for health, to lose some unwanted pounds, to finally release your part in the violence inflicted on our animals, to leave a smaller footprint on our yearning planet, or some combination of any or all of these noble reasons, we welcome you with open arms. Just do us this one favor: please leave all judgment for yourself and others at the door. Step into today, into your new life where

strength is in the moment—the food you are eating at each meal; the walk or run you took this morning; your daily yoga practice; and the individual choices you make in each moment.

As you journey through life, remember that you always have the power to alter your current experience by taking action to shift your perspective away from past events and future projections and to anchor in the present. The now moment will always help you become reborn and renewed. It's the secret to transcending anything. Here's how to access it: drawing attention to the breath, take a long, deep inhale followed by a long, deep exhale. It's as simple as that. Notice your anxiety wane as you connect with deep peace and greater awareness. Now breathe all of that in and know that you are loved simply for your presence, the way you are right now, in this moment.

A LOVING HONEST DIALOGUE ABOUT THE
CONSEQUENCES OF FOOD CHOICE CREATES

THE SPACE FOR A FREEDOM OF EXPLORATION
AND A SUSTAINABLE HEALTHY LIFESTYLE.

LATTES
+ TEAS

TRANSFORM YOUR LATTES & TEAS . . .

Don't give up your lattes and teas; instead, transform them! Using superfoods, nut milks, and healthy natural sweeteners in your warm morning liquids instead of the usual dairy, processed sugar, and excess caffeine is a game changer. Getting creative by using healthy ingredients will take you far in your quest for vibrant health. Why overspend at your local coffee house? Preparing unique, superior-tasting, and far healthier versions at home does both your body and budget right.

The true beauty of the early morning is embodied in the steaming waters of lattes and teas. The rich satisfying taste of a creamy latte enlivens the senses. The expanded silence of late-evening moments is revealed in the Zen of tea. These comforting warm liquids can take many forms. In this section, we offer unique, upgraded varieties to please the palate—free from harsh stimulants and toxins and intended to nurture the soul and nourish the body temple.

Teeming with nutrients, these drinks provide a sustained, even-keeled energy that lasts throughout your day. Whether it's in the healing of the turmeric, the rawness of the cacao, or the digestive fire in the ginger, enjoy our fresh new twist on these warm drinks made with creamy, frothy nut and seed milks. And don't forget to absorb the beauty of fresh healing herbal teas sweetened with raw, sustainably harvested honey.

This is "The Plantpower Way" home.

LATTES

These recipes take only minutes to make, just a bit longer than boiling a teakettle on the stove. I highly recommend taking the time to select a special cup you enjoy holding in your hands. One of the great pleasures of life is a favorite tea mug. I prefer handmade ceramics—an earthy element to ground my latte ritual. You will also need a strainer, some fine cheesecloth, or a nut milk bag. Our lattes make for an authentic café experience in the comfort of your own home.

Cacao Date Cashew Latte

The best hot chocolate ever! I tend to use hemp seeds and cashews for my nut milks because they blend up smooth and creamy and don't require straining. Sweetened with fresh dates, this combination is a cup of chocolaty goodness.

Ingredients

• 2 cups boiling water
• ½ cup raw cashews
• 2 tablespoons raw cacao powder
• 2 dates, pitted

Preparation

1. Bring the water to a boil on the stove.

2. To a Vitamix or high-powered blender, add the cashews, cacao powder, dates, and boiling water. Blend on high for a full minute.

3. Pour through a cheesecloth or strainer, if desired. Serve.

Mocha Latte

A creamy blend of cacao and coffee topped with a velvety layer of nut milk froth. Brazil nuts are high in skin-healing vitamin E and testosterone-boosting selenium. To ensure a smooth consistency, strain the nuts and cacao nibs through a fine sieve or cheesecloth. Enjoy this enlivening latte in a quiet morning hour.

Ingredients

• 4 cups organic fresh-brewed coffee (regular or decaf)
• ¼ vanilla bean
• 5 organic Brazil nuts
• 2 teaspoons cacao nibs
• 1 teaspoon raw honey
• Dash cinnamon

Preparation

1. Brew a pot of your favorite coffee.

2. Split the vanilla bean lengthwise and scrape out the seeds.

3. Add all the ingredients to a Vitamix or high-powered blender. Blend on high for a full minute.

4. Strain the mixture through cheesecloth or a fine strainer.

5. Pour into your favorite cup.

6. For an iced version, add 3 cups ice and blend again.

Ginger Turmeric Latte

Two miracle roots unite to form this magical healing latte. Frothy, rich, and delicious, this anti-inflammatory elixir will soothe your mind and your stomach. Ginger works wonders for digestion while the nutrient-rich hemp seeds blend to give you a nice and creamy protein-packed drink. Wrap your hands around this delight and let the healing begin.

Ingredients

- 2 cups water
- 1" piece fresh ginger, peeled
- 1" piece fresh turmeric root, peeled
- ¼ cup hemp seeds
- 1 teaspoon raw honey
- Dash cardamom

Preparation

1. Bring the water to a boil on the stove.

2. Using a fine hand grater, grate both the ginger and turmeric.

3. Add all the ingredients, except the cardamom, plus the boiling water, to a Vitamix or high-powered blender. Blend on high for 1 minute.

4. Pour the mixture through cheesecloth or a fine strainer and serve. Garnish with a sprinkle of cardamom.

TEA LATTES

Lighter than a latte but heartier than an herbal tea. These aromatic, flavorful elixirs are a natural bridge between a classic latte and a regular hot tea. For centuries, tea has been recognized for its healing properties and effectively used in alternative medicine to treat and heal many ailments. Experiment with these blends to discover your personal equilibrium.

Vanilla Chai Latte

There is something wonderfully potent and mysterious about the ancient, spicy flavor and savory aroma of this morning blend, a gentle way to ease into the early dawn. Give this vanilla latte a try and experience a little piece of India.

Ingredients

- 6 cups filtered water
- 1 teaspoon coconut oil
- ½" vanilla bean
- 12 whole green cardamom pods
- 12 whole black peppercorns
- 2 cinnamon sticks
- 3 black tea bags
- 1 cup fresh Sweet Vanilla Almond Milk (page 75)
- 6 teaspoons coconut or date sugar

Preparation

1. In a medium saucepan, add all the ingredients except the almond milk and coconut sugar. Bring to a boil over high heat, then reduce the heat and simmer for 15 minutes.

2. Turn off the heat, remove the tea bags, and strain into individual cups.

3. To each individual cup, add almond milk and raw coconut sugar to taste. Namaste!

Mint Honey Hemp Latte

Hemp seeds are the secret to making a quick and easy frothy milk brimming over with superpowered nutrients. Rife with protein and essential fatty acids, these tiny seeds work wonders for your health! This blend of fresh mint and honey creates a unique flavor combination. Make this herbal offering and find a comfortable seat to sip, relax, and unwind.

Ingredients

- Boiling water
- 1 bunch fresh mint leaves
- 2 tablespoons hemp seeds
- 1½ cups filtered water
- 2 teaspoons raw honey

Preparation

1. Fill a teapot with boiling water and steep the mint leaves, reserving a few for garnish, for about 8 minutes.

2. In a Vitamix or high-powered blender, blend the hemp seeds in the filtered water for a full minute.

3. Pour the tea into your favorite cup to three-quarters full; top off with frothy hemp milk. Drizzle a teaspoon of honey over the top and garnish with a mint leaf. *OM.*

HERBAL TEAS

The morning tea ritual is a beautiful opportunity to engage all your senses with nature. Unfortunately, we have become so used to buying tea bags from the store, we often forget the most aromatic and soothing teas exist right in our herb gardens. Anyone can have an herb basket growing near the kitchen. All you have to do is pick a bunch of fresh herbs, then steep them in a teapot with boiling water for about eight minutes. If you prefer, you can just place the herbs in the bottom of your cup and fill it with boiling water. If desired, sweeten these herbal teas with raw local honey or coconut sugar.

Fresh Mint

Truly one of my favorite herbs. This is a great, calming tea after dinner as it soothes indigestion. I like mine with a teaspoon of local raw honey.

Promotes digestion and protection from illness.

Lemongrass

My friend June makes the most divine tea with lemongrass fresh from her garden. It has a mild lemony taste. Lemongrass aids digestion and relieves cramping. You have to remove and discard the outside greener leaves first, then use the light yellow inside sections to make the tea.

Releases anger, resentment, and regret.

Rose

There is nothing quite like rose tea. I drink it when I need a little tenderness in my life. I also love to drink it when I am meditating in the early morning, as it doesn't disturb my serenity. You will need the petals from about ten roses.

For gratitude and simplicity.

Chamomile

Fresh chamomile from the garden makes a beautiful tea. Well known for its calming and medicinal properties, this tea is a powerful sleep aid. You'll need a nice bunch to make the tea strong enough, so use more than you think is necessary. Steep it in a teapot, but save some of the sweet, white, daisy-like flowers for a garnish in your tea. Chamomile is best without any sweetener or milk.

A natural calming medicine.

FIND YOUR TRUE HOME

THE PLACE WHERE YOU ARE EATING TO LIVE AND LOVING IT.

TREATS +
SWEETS

THE SWEET LIFE

A plant-based lifestyle doesn't require you to abandon the sweetness of life in the foods you enjoy. It just requires a little reorientation in the way you think about and use everyone's favorite taste.

Give Me Some Sugar... Unrefined

Without a doubt, processed, highly refined sugars like high-fructose corn syrup are significantly damaging to our body's intricate systems. More and more research points to sugar as a primary culprit in a vast array of chronic ailments and diseases. Further complicating matters is our widespread cultural addiction to this diabolical substance, which somehow finds its way into every processed food imaginable. The worst part? Most of us are completely unaware of just how much sugar we ingest daily.

The American Heart Association (AHA) advises no more than 9.5 teaspoons of sugar per day—high if you ask me or the World Health Organization (WHO), which recently recommended no more than 5 percent of all calories come from sugar intake. But for American children, it seems every day is Halloween. The typical American kid averages about 32 teaspoons of sugar daily. The average teenager consumes the sugar equivalent of 18 fun-size candies every single day!

Beyond the fact that sugar contains no essential nutrients, excessive consumption is inextricably linked to the increased incidence and onset of chronic disease, including cancer, liver disease, obesity, diabetes, and heart disease, America's number one killer. In fact, some studies suggest that high sugar consumption just might double your chances of dying from a heart attack. Scary stuff indeed.

But let's be clear. We're not asking you to give up those amazing pies that Grandma baked nor the kids' favorite peanut butter cookies. We don't believe in depriving our family the love that permeates our home-style cooking. What we do believe in is shifting how we sweeten and prepare our desserts, using healthier whole-food plant-based alternatives to upgrade recipes traditionally reliant upon heavy doses of refined sugar, eggs, and butter. Done right, you can still create amazing-tasting love offerings soon to become new and nutritious family traditions.

Here's my basic approach when it comes to sweetening our family creations:

Date Me

Dates are a highly nutritious complete whole food. Known to promote heart, bone, and digestive health, dates are packed with fiber; nutritious antioxidants; essential minerals including potassium, magnesium, and copper; and vitamins including A and K.

Our friend and longevity expert Dan Buettner is the author of the best-selling book **The Blue Zones**, a primer on the lifestyles and diets that characterize the world's longest-living and happiest cultures. He is also a renowned ultra-athlete with three world records for endurance cycling. He recently told us that he rode his bike across the Sahara on nothing but dates and water. Dan was amazed at how well this simple food sustained his body under protracted, grueling conditions. If dates could fortify him across such a scorched, infertile wilderness, then imagine what they can do for you. Did I mention that dates also taste amazing? For all these reasons and more, dates top my list of favorite sweet foods. They're great served plain as a simple snack on the go. They're perfect to accompany your next workout; Rich *always* grabs a handful for his rides. They're ideal for smoothie blends. And they're superb when it comes to creating amazing desserts!

Be Fruitful

Use a bounty of whole fruits and fresh-pressed fruit juices created for us by Mother Nature whenever possible. Fruits not only add sweetness; they provide plenty of fiber, phytonutrients, micronutrients, antioxidants, minerals, and vitamins. Freshen your meals with a garnish of pineapple, apple, grapes, or blueberries. For dessert, a smoothie blend of exotic fruits, a creamy banana shake, or homemade coconut and fruit ice cream trumps store-bought treats any day.

Aw, Honey, Honey

A powerful, healing superfood that nourishes our bodies in miraculous ways, raw unprocessed honey is the food of the mystical bees—masters of service and community. The ancients believed honey to be the nectar of the gods. Astoundingly, honey found in the ancient tombs of Egypt has maintained its composition over thousands of years. Cancer fighting and anti-allergenic, honey deserves its superfood moniker. Manuka honey can even be applied topically to treat infections, bites, and cuts as a powerful antibacterial! Relatively low on the glycemic index, we love honey in a myriad of desserts that grace the pages of this section.

However, it is crucial to understand that mass pesticide use, loss of habitat, unsustainable commercial beekeeping practices, and many other factors have contributed to an alarming decline in global bee populations. In the United States alone, 30 percent of the bee population and nearly a third of all bee colonies have perished—*and that's just in the last five years!* The global environmental implications of this are staggering. For this reason, as well as ethical concerns, pure vegans completely abstain from honey, which is a beautiful and noble action to take. We feel the best way to help the bees thrive is to bring them closer into our community by supporting local sustainable beekeepers who practice conscious awareness when harvesting honey from the hives. The lion's share of honey is always left for the bees. When production is low, none should be taken.

Becoming beekeepers ourselves and/or supporting local beekeepers in utilizing natural, pesticide-free, noninvasive practices should be a high priority. Here are four ways you can help support our powerful pollinators:

1. Buy local organic honey from beekeepers who practice conscious methods.

2. Plant a pollinator garden.

3. Become a beekeeper or hang out with one. We frequent local hives, which is a great educational opportunity for our kids. Honoring, nurturing, learning from, and interacting with our pollinator friends and their stewards deepens our understanding of the crucial role they play in the health of our global ecology.

4. Connect with the bees spiritually. Bees remind us to extract the honey of life. Pollination is a potent metaphor for the inherent power of spreading love and service for the betterment of all. The honeycomb hexagon is a symbol of the heart, representing the sweetness of life found within all of us.

5. Finally, when you take that spoonful of sweet honey, take a moment to remember what an extraordinary gift this superfood is. Let's all join with the bees and nurture them with our conscious care and love!

Maple Syrup

Although maple syrup is admittedly processed, it comes from trees and adds some great vibrational qualities to our recipes. With more minerals than honey, this golden nectar will boost your immune system, reduce inflammation, calm tummy troubles, and even age-proof your skin. Expand your use of maple syrup beyond pancakes and waffles. Used in moderation, it's great in oatmeal, baked goods, and pies. Try drizzling a smidge over a baked yam!

Agave, Stevia & Raw Sugars

Avoid. Stevia is highly processed, soon to be genetically modified, and doesn't work well with baking. Hyped as a health food, agave nectars are also highly processed and actually higher in fructose than high-fructose corn syrup itself. However, I occasionally and sparingly use organic raw sugar in a few recipes where I can't get a substitution to deliver the consistency I am striving for. Don't judge me. As we evolve, our techniques will shift and advance. One step at a time.

Artificial Sweeteners

Never. Period.

PEANUT BUTTER COOKIES

8–12

Easily our all-time favorite cookies. Trapper is our family's master cookie chef. He likes to roll them into 1½"-diameter balls and then press them flat using the tines of a fork to make a nice space for the chocolate square. The texture will vary depending upon the brand of peanut butter used. The cookie dough should stick together like play dough when pressed. If you find your dough crumbling, add water in increments of 1 tablespoon. If it's sticky, add ground flaxseeds in increments of 1 tablespoon. In a word, perfection!

Ingredients

- 1 teaspoon coconut oil
- 2 tablespoons ground flaxseeds
- ¼ cup filtered water
- 1 cup organic, natural-style crunchy peanut butter
- 1¼ cups organic sugar
- 2 teaspoons high-quality vanilla extract
- 1 bar Mayan dark chocolate or high-quality organic specialty chocolate (vegan)
- 1 teaspoon large-grain Celtic sea salt

Preparation

1. Preheat the oven to 350°F and grease a cookie sheet with the coconut oil using a paper towel.

2. To make a flaxseed egg, mix the ground flaxseeds and the filtered water. Let stand for 2 minutes and then whisk until the mixture has an egg-like texture. Add more filtered water as needed to get the consistency of an egg.

3. In a medium bowl, mix the peanut butter and sugar, flaxseed "egg," and vanilla with clean hands until well combined.

4. Roll 1½ tablespoons of the mixture into smooth balls and place about 1" apart on the prepared baking sheet.

5. Press flat using a fork, making a lined pattern on the cookies.

6. Press one square of dark chocolate in the center of each cookie. Strategically place large sea salt crystals on top of the cookies.

7. Bake, until golden around the edges, 10 to 12 minutes. Let cool until they are slightly warm. Carefully transfer to a serving plate using a spatula.

8. Devour.

ABUELA'S GLAZED BANANAS

2-4

This is a Chilean family recipe that has stood the test of time. When I was a child, my mother prepared this dish for us as a warm topping to be served over vanilla ice cream. It was always delicious! Today my mother is "La Abuela" to ten grandchildren and four great-grandchildren. Her tasty glazed bananas continue to nourish generation after generation. A favorite in our house, this dish is incredibly simple, fast, tasty, and versatile. Serve it traditionally over a version of our Coconut Ice Cream (page 266), try these bananas with our Supersoulfood Pancakes (page 141) in the morning, or serve them as a side to our Tempeh Chili (page 165).

Ingredients

- 4 firm bananas
- ½ teaspoon coconut oil
- ¼ cup maple syrup
- 1 teaspoon cinnamon

Preparation

1. Peel and slice the bananas in half lengthwise down the middle.

2. In a medium saucepan, heat the coconut oil and tilt the pan to coat the bottom.

3. On medium-low heat, sauté the bananas until they slightly soften. Turn them over and repeat. Remove from the heat.

4. Drizzle the maple syrup over the bananas and sprinkle with the cinnamon.

MANGO PIE

The creation of this pie was inspired by the magical island of Kauai, which provided the most exquisite, sweet-perfumed mangos for the filling the first time I made it. The exotic mango has a unique taste like no other fruit and it is also a wonderful source of fiber; vitamins A, B_6, C, and E; potassium; and flavonoids like beta-carotene. If the mango is very sweet, you may not need any additional sweeteners. Enjoy the happy blend of tropical colors and flavors with the buttery taste of macadamia and cashew nuts. This dessert is the essence of Kauai in one perfect pie.

Ingredients

CRUST

- 8 dates
- Filtered water
- 1½ cups macadamia nuts
- Pinch Celtic sea salt
- 1 teaspoon coconut oil

FILLING

- 4 cups frozen mango
- 1½ cups raw cashews, soaked in filtered water
- 2 cups shredded coconut, plus more for garnish
- ½ cup raw honey (optional)

Preparation

1. Soak the dates in filtered water for at least 30 minutes. Remove the pits and set aside.

2. In a food processor, pulse the macadamia nuts until mealy in texture.

3. Add the Celtic sea salt and pulse again.

4. With the motor running, drop the soaked pitted dates in one at a time until the dough balls up on the side of the bowl.

5. Lightly oil a 9" springform pan with coconut oil. Press the nut/date mixture into the bottom of the pan evenly. Place in the freezer.

6. To a Vitamix or high-powered blender, add the mango, soaked cashews, and shredded coconut. Blend on high until the mixture is smooth.

7. Pour into the springform pan and freeze for at least 2 hours. Remove from the freezer 30 minutes before serving and garnish with coconut pieces.

Chef's Note: If you use a 13" springform pan, double the pie ingredients. If you can't find macadamia nuts, feel free to substitute cashews or Brazil nuts (unsoaked) for the crust.

LAVENDER LEMON BALLS

6–8

These raw treats are some of my favorites. I use lavender and lemons picked fresh from our garden. Like aromatic offerings of love, each bite really satisfies the sweet cravings of my soul. Before our home was built I would walk our land, absorbing the waft of lemon trees and lavender fields. No matter where I find myself, these country smells always make me feel like I'm home.

Ingredients

- 1 cup raw cashews
- 2 tablespoons hemp seeds
- 1 cup almond flour
- 1 tablespoon fresh lavender from your garden or farmers' market
- 2 tablespoons fresh lemon rind
- ½ cup raw local honey
- Lavender blooms, for garnish

Preparation

1. In a food processor, pulse the cashews until mealy in texture. Add the hemp seeds and pulse a few more times.

2. Add the almond flour, lavender, and lemon rind. Pulse again 6 times.

3. With the motor running, add the honey until a ball forms on one side of the bowl.

4. Roll the dough into 1" balls and arrange on a serving plate.

5. Store in the refrigerator until ready to serve.

6. Garnish with fresh lavender blooms.

COCONUT ICE CREAMS

The delicious dairy-free ice cream revolution is upon us. Coconut ice creams are so creamy and full bodied, you'll swear they contain milk. Depending on the ripeness of the fruit, you may even decide to skip the sweetener! If we do sweeten, we prefer raw honey but you can use maple syrup or dates if you like. Try serving these creations mounded inside a whole fruit like a cracked coconut half or a scooped-out orange or lemon.

Coconut Ginger

Sweet creamy coconut, aromatic mango, and lively ginger make this ice cream an absolute delight. Ginger is perfect at the end of a meal to aid digestion and has great anti-inflammatory properties. The sweetness from the mango and honey make this dessert an offering from the gods.

Ingredients

- 1 (15-ounce) can coconut cream
- 10 ounces frozen mango
- ½ teaspoon cardamom, plus more for garnish
- ½" piece ginger, peeled
- ¼ cup raw clear honey

Preparation

1. Put the coconut cream in the fridge for a few hours or overnight. I store a few cans in the fridge instead of the pantry so they are always ready for a quick batch of ice cream.

2. Open the can, scoop out the hardened coconut cream, and discard the liquid.

3. Add the coconut cream and frozen mango to your Vitamix or high-powered blender. Blend on medium speed, using the plunger consistently on all sides to blend the frozen fruit and the coconut evenly.

4. When it is smooth, add the cardamom, ginger, and raw honey. Blend again for 30 seconds.

5. For a beautiful presentation, scoop the ice cream inside half of a cracked coconut shell. Freeze until firm (about 2 hours). Sprinkle with cardamom and serve.

Mexican Chocolate

Calling all chocolate lovers out there, this version is the flavor bomb. So many wonderful flavors melding into a decadent tribe of tasty! Enjoy the many health benefits of raw cacao, full of magnesium, fiber, iron, and antioxidants. This dish is a great way to boost nutrition without depriving yourself of a delicious dessert. *¡Ole!* Baby . . .

Ingredients

- 1 (15-ounce) can coconut cream, chilled
- 2 frozen bananas, peeled
- 2 tablespoons cacao powder
- ½ cup cacao nibs
- ½ cup raw clear honey, blue agave, or maple syrup
- ½ teaspoon cinnamon
- ¼ teaspoon cayenne pepper

Preparation

1. Open the can and scoop out the hardened coconut cream right into the Vitamix or food processor. Make sure you leave the liquid behind in the can. (Or use it to prepare your own fresh Coconut Honey Cream, page 80).

2. Add the frozen bananas, cacao powder, cacao nibs, honey, cinnamon, and cayenne.

3. Blend on medium speed, using the plunger to distribute the ingredients evenly until the mixture is smooth.

4. Transfer the mixture to a rectangular glass dish and freeze. When the ice cream has hardened, serve up a luscious mound with an ice cream scooper.

recipe continues >>

Pink Raspberry

Keeping it simple and pretty in pink. The brilliant color of real raspberries makes this coconut cream concoction really pop. Serving up more than just a pretty color, raspberries pack a powerful punch of antioxidants, phytonutrients, iron, potassium, zinc, and fiber to round out this delight.

Ingredients

- 1 (15-ounce) can coconut cream, chilled
- 10 ounces frozen raspberries
- ¼ cup raw clear honey or light agave

Preparation

1. Open the can, scoop out the hardened coconut cream, and discard the liquid (or use it to prepare your own fresh Coconut Honey Cream, page 80).

2. Add the coconut cream, frozen raspberries, and honey to the Vitamix or food processor and blend until the mixture is smooth.

3. Transfer into pretty serving bowls and freeze for 1 to 2 hours, or until it's firm.

CACAO MINT AVOCADO TART

8-10

This flavorful tart is a chocolate lover's dream where mint and chocolate unite to form the most indulgent yet nutritious dessert. Avocado is one of nature's most nutrient-packed fruits, wonderful for your heart and skin, and cacao is loaded with antioxidants. Walnuts are the perfect brain food and may even increase your life span and lower your risk of cancer. So what's stopping you? *Be the baker!*

Ingredients

CRUST

- 8 dates, pitted
- Filtered water
- 1 teaspoon coconut oil
- 1½ cups raw walnuts
- ½ cup cacao nibs
- Pinch Celtic sea salt

FILLING

- 2 small avocados, peeled and pitted
- 1 cup soaked cashews
- 1 (15-ounce) can whole coconut milk
- ½ cup light agave or raw honey
- ¼ cup cacao powder
- ½ cup cacao nibs
- Juice of 1 lemon
- 1 whole vanilla bean
- 2 cups packed fresh mint leaves, plus leaves for garnish

recipe continues >>

Preparation

1. In a small bowl, soak the dates in filtered water for 30 minutes. Grease the springform pan with the cocount oil and set aside.

2. In a food processor, pulse the walnuts until mealy in texture. Add the cacao nibs and sea salt. Process for 15 seconds.

3. With the motor running, add the soaked dates one at a time until the mixture forms a ball on one side of the bowl. You may have to stop the processor, redistribute the mixture, and pulse again until the dates are well incorporated.

4. In the oiled springform pan, press the crust mixture into the base to form an even layer on the bottom. Place in the freezer for 10 to 12 minutes, until firm.

5. Meanwhile, prepare the filling: place the avocados, cashews, coconut milk, agave, cacao powder, cacao nibs, lemon juice, vanilla bean, and mint leaves (on top) in a Vitamix or high-powered blender.

6. Using the plunger, distribute the mint into the mixture as you blend on low speed. Keep at it until the mint is well incorporated and then increase the speed to thoroughly puree the mixture. The consistency should be custard-like.

7. Taste to adjust the sweetness and add more agave or honey, if needed.

8. Remove the crust from the freezer and pour the filling into the pan. Using a spatula, distribute the custard evenly and smooth the surface.

9. Return to the freezer for at least 2 hours.

10. Thaw for 30 minutes prior to serving. Garnish with fresh mint and enjoy!

11. This pie can be stored in the refrigerator or freezer for 4 to 7 days.

Chef's Note: Adjust the taste for sweetness. You shouldn't be able to taste the avocados. If the avocado taste is prominent, then add more sweetener in increments of ¼ cup. You can also add a squeeze of lemon to neutralize the avocado flavor.

CHIA LIME PIE

Lime, coconut, and chia seeds remind me of our island adventures living in the tropics. I created this pie in our yurt kitchen lab on the North Shore of Kauai in between teaching yoga classes at Common Ground. Whole foods like chia seeds, walnuts, fresh coconut, and lime juice make a delicious combination for a healthy dessert packed with plenty of plant-sourced omega-3 fats, protein, calcium, antioxidants, and magnesium.

Ingredients

CRUST

- 1 teaspoon coconut oil
- 1½ cups raw walnuts
- ½ teaspoon Celtic sea salt
- 8 dates, soaked in filtered water for about 30 minutes and pitted
- 1 lime

FILLING

- 1½ cups raw cashews, soaked overnight in filtered water
- 1½ cups fresh coconut meat
- ¼ cup chia seeds in ¾ cup water
- 1 tablespoon soy or sunflower lecithin
- 1 teaspoon vanilla extract
- 2 tablespoons coconut oil
- 1 (15-ounce) can coconut cream
- 3 small limes
- ½ cup light agave or raw honey
- 1 lime, cut into wedges, for garnish
- Mint leaves, for garnish

Preparation

1. Lightly grease a 9" springform pan with the coconut oil.

2. In a food processor, pulse the walnuts until they are mealy in consistency.

3. Add the sea salt. Pulse again to combine.

4. Add the dates one at a time through the tube of the food processor until well incorporated. You may need to stop the blade and scrape down the sides a couple of times.

5. In the oiled springform pan, press the nut-date mixture along the bottom to form the base crust. Grate the zest from the lime to cover the crust. Place the crust in the freezer.

6. In a Vitamix or high-powered blender, process the cashews and the coconut meat and blend.

7. Add the soaked chia seeds (which should have become gelatinous), lecithin, vanilla, coconut oil, and coconut cream and blend well.

8. Squeeze the limes into the processor and blend again. Then add the agave or honey to taste and blend one more time.

9. Remove the crust from the freezer and pour the filling into the springform pan. Smooth the top with a spatula.

10. Freeze for 2 hours, until it's set and firm.

11. Thaw the pie for 30 minutes prior to serving. Garnish with fresh lime wedges and mint before serving.

6–8

VEGAN PUMPKIN PIE

This is such a favorite around our home that our kids beg me to make it all year round. I highly recommend baking your own pumpkin as it really does increase the nutrition and overall quality of the pie. Pure pumpkin is loaded with immunity-boosting beta-carotene, which the body converts into a form of vitamin A. It's also an often overlooked source of fiber. Adding sorghum flour to the crust gives it more of a traditional flaky texture and crunchy walnuts add those heart-healthy omega-3 fats. Using silken tofu will give the pie filling a very smooth texture. If you use sprouted tofu, expect the filling to be more grainy in consistency. You can make this pie as a raw, frozen dessert or go classic and bake it in the oven. We vary our preparation depending on the season and who is seated at our dinner table. Mathis likes it cooked; Tyler likes it raw. Both versions are amazing.

Ingredients

CRUST

- 1 teaspoon coconut oil
- 1½ cups raw walnuts
- ½ cup ground flaxseeds
- ½ cup sorghum flour
- 8 dates, soaked in filtered water for about 30 minutes and pitted
- 1 bag dried beans (to be used as pie weights only for a cooked crust)

FILLING

- 2 small pumpkins, seeded, baked, and skins removed (about 2 cups)
- 1 (12-ounce) package silken tofu
- ¼ cup coconut cream
- 1 cup maple syrup
- ½ teaspoon nutmeg
- ½ teaspoon cinnamon
- Juice of ½ lemon

TOPPING

- Cashew Vanilla Cream (page 81)

Preparation

1. For a raw pie, lightly grease a 9" springform pan with the coconut oil. For a cooked pie, lightly grease a 9" glass pie plate.

2. In a food processor, pulse the walnuts until mealy in texture. Add the flaxseed and sorghum flour and continue to pulse a few more times.

3. With the motor running, add the dates one at a time until the mixture balls up on one side of the processor and forms a dough.

4. For a raw pie, press the dough evenly into the prepared springform pan to form your crust. Place in the freezer for 10 to 12 minutes, or until firm.

For a cooked pie, press the dough into the prepared glass pie plate. Weight down with dried beans and prebake at 325°F for 10 minutes. Then remove the dried beans, and raise the oven temperature to 350°F.

5. In a Vitamix or high-powered blender, add the filling ingredients and blend until smooth. Remove the crust from the freezer (for a raw pie) and pour in the filling into your choice of crust.

6. For a raw pie, return it to the freezer for a minimum of 2 hours or until it hardens. Let it thaw for 30 minutes before serving.

For a cooked pie, bake it for 40 minutes at 350°F or until it sets up well. You will need to cool it completely before cutting.

7. Top with a layer of Cashew Vanilla Cream.

Chef's Note: If you use a 13" springform pan, double the pie ingredients. For a cooked pie, remember the dried beans are just to weigh down the crust to prevent the dough from rising when you prebake it. Remove the beans before you pour in the filling.

STRAWBERRY MINT CACAO CHEESECAKE

The people have spoken! Rich's photo of this pie received our most "likes" to date on Instagram. The combination of real fruit, powerful herbs, and raw cacao takes this plantpowered cheesecake to a whole new level. The cacao, coconut, fruit, and mint provide a nice variety of antioxidants, vitamins, and fiber that will heal your body. Raw pies are so easy to make that once you get the hang of it, you'll fancy yourself the family baker. Shhh! Don't tell anyone. You won't really be baking anything at all because the magic happens in the freezer. But we'll keep that as our little secret. The one tool you are going to need is a great springform pan. There you have it!

Ingredients

CRUST

- 1 teaspoon coconut oil
- 1½ cups raw walnuts
- 1 cup cacao nibs
- 8 dates, soaked in filtered water for 30 minutes and pitted
- ½ teaspoon Celtic sea salt

FILLING

- 1 (15-ounce) can whole coconut milk
- 8 dates
- 1 pint fresh strawberries
- 1 cup raw coconut meat
- ¼ cup cacao powder
- 1 cup packed fresh mint leaves

- 1 tablespoon soy or sunflower lecithin
- Agave, raw honey, or maple syrup
- Edible flower or mint leaf, for garnish

GARNISH

- 2 pints fresh strawberries
- Fresh mint leaves

Preparation

1. Place a can of coconut milk in the fridge overnight or for at least 2 hours. (It's a great idea to have a few cans stocked in your fridge. If you're like me, you may get the urge to make a pie in the middle of the night, and this way, you'll be prepared.)

2. For the crust, pour the coconut oil into a 9" springform pan. Using a paper towel or clean cloth, wipe the oil over the bottom and sides of the pan. Set aside.

3. In a food processor, pulse the walnuts until they are mealy in texture. Add the cacao nibs and pulse again until they are mixed in. With the motor running, drop in one date at a time until the mixture forms a ball on one side.

recipe continues >>

You may have to remove the lid and redistribute the mixture a couple of times to get all the dates blended in.

4. Press the crust mixture into the bottom of the springform pan using flat hands to create an even crust layer. Sprinkle sea salt over the crust. Place in the freezer.

5. Remove the coconut milk from the fridge and open it. Spoon out the hardened coconut cream, discarding the liquid in the bottom of the can.

6. Place all the filling ingredients into a Vitamix or high-powered blender. Blend on high, using the plunger to distribute the mixture to blend smoothly. Taste to adjust for sweetness. You can add ¼ cup

agave, raw honey, maple syrup, or a few more dates if needed to sweeten it up.

7. Pour the blended filling mixture into the crust and freeze again for at least 2 hours, or until it is very firm.

8. Remove the pie from the freezer. Carefully run a fine knife around the edges of the springform and release the buckle. Slowly remove the rim, allowing it to separate from the pie. Place it on a serving platter. Now you are ready to begin creating your strawberry mandala.

9. To make that super-impressive swirl on top, slice the 2 pints of strawberries lengthwise. Begin on the outer edge and lay the strawberry slices with the tips pointing out from the center. When you finish an entire layer around the outside edge, begin the next layer so it lies partly on top of your base layer. Continue just like that, around and around, until you arrive at the center.

10. Garnish with a fresh flower or a mint leaf in the center. Thaw this pie at room temperature for 30 minutes before serving. *Magnifique!*

Chef's Note: If you use a 13" springform pan, double the filling ingredients.

You can use a processor or blender other than a Vitamix for this recipe. However, the mixture will not be as smooth. You may find little bits of date and coconut that will yield a more grainy texture.

Using soy or sunflower lecithin in any of my raw pies will bind the oils and make the pie filling set up like a firm custard. This allows it to hold up in the refrigerator after you have cut slices. I only use it if I think there will be leftovers, which is rare in my house.

PEACH BLUEBERRY HIGH (PIE)

6–8

This lovely spring pie was created when I was cooking for a group of twenty-five yogis at my friend Saul Raye's Thai Yoga retreat in Ojai, California. When I finished arranging the peach slices in a spiral, I was left with a large opening in the center. My daughter Mathis had the idea to place a bunch of blueberries in the center. It worked beautifully! When the pie was fresh out of the oven, a didgeridoo player joined me in the kitchen and I asked him to infuse the pie with sound. This beautiful pie will infuse your soul and make your heart sing for more.

Ingredients

FILLING

- 7 peaches, pitted and sliced into wedges (skins on)
- 1 cup organic sugar
- 1 tablespoon cinnamon
- 1 tablespoon plus 1 teaspoon tapioca flour
- 10 ounces frozen blueberries, completely thawed, excess liquid drained

CRUST

- 1 teaspoon coconut oil
- 1½ cups raw almonds, soaked overnight
- Pinch Celtic sea salt
- 10 dates, soaked in filtered water for 30 minutes and pitted

Preparation

1. Preheat the oven to 350°F.

2. In a bowl, combine the sliced peaches, sugar, cinnamon, and 1 tablespoon tapioca flour. With clean hands, gently fold the peaches over until they are well coated. Set aside.

3. Lightly grease a 9" springform pan with coconut oil. In a food processor, pulse the almonds until mealy in texture. Add the sea salt and pulse again.

4. With the motor running, add the dates one at a time until the mixture forms a dough on the side of the bowl.

5. Using your palms, press the dough evenly into the bottom of the prepared pan.

6. Atop the dough, arrange the peaches in a circular pattern, starting on the outside of the pan and working your way toward the inside, overlapping the sections as you go. Keep layering until you have three rows and a large round opening in the center.

7. Toss the blueberries with the remaining teaspoon of tapioca flour and then arrange in the opening.

8. Bake for 20 to 30 minutes or until the fruit begins to bubble. Remove from the oven and let cool.

Chef's Note: Baking this pie for a shorter time preserves more of the nutrients and leaves the peaches tasting fresh and crisp.

6

MEXICAN CACAO BROWNIES

The cinnamon and dark chocolate chili give this brownie a fun Mexican fiesta flair. With layers of flavor in every moist bite, you will embark on an expedition of taste and discovery. Once again these brownies score high on our health scale with antioxidant-rich dark chocolate and cacao. The kids plow through these as a special dessert or snack to share with friends. As with all gluten-free baked treats, they will retain their shape better if you allow them to cool fully before cutting.

Ingredients

- 3 tablespoons ground flaxseeds
- 6 tablespoons filtered water
- Coconut oil, for greasing
- ¾ cup garbanzo flour
- ¼ cup tapioca flour
- ½ cup cacao powder
- ¼ teaspoon baking soda
- ¾ teaspoon xanthan gum
- ½ teaspoon Celtic sea salt
- 1 teaspoon cinnamon
- 1 cup almond meal
- 1 (3.5-ounce) high-quality dark chocolate chili bar
- 1¼ cups organic cane sugar
- 1 cup plus 2 tablespoons vegan butter (Earth Balance)
- ½ cup unsweetened almond milk
- 1 teaspoon vanilla
- 9 ounces vegan chocolate chips

Preparation

1. In a small bowl, whisk together the ground flaxseeds and filtered water until the mixture forms an egg-like consistency.

2. Preheat the oven to 350°F.

3. Line the bottom of a 9" square pan with parchment paper and lightly oil the sides with coconut oil. Set aside.

4. In a large bowl, sift together the garbanzo flour, tapioca flour, cacao powder, baking soda, xanthan gum, sea salt, and cinnamon. Add the almond meal and stir with a wooden spoon.

5. Create a double boiler by bringing water to a boil in a small saucepan. Rest a small metal bowl over the top of the pan, add the chocolate bar, and let sit until it's melted. Stir occasionally.

6. In a mixer with the paddle attachment, add the sugar, 2 tablespoons vegan butter, flaxseed "egg," almond milk, and vanilla. Mix until smooth.

7. Add the melted chocolate and mix again.

8. Making a well in the center of the dry ingredients, pour the wet ingredients into the dry, and mix well with a rubber spatula. The mixture should be thick and gooey. If it is too dry, you can add a very small amount of almond milk, 1 tablespoon at a time. However, it should be perfect!

9. Fold in three-quarters of the bag of chocolate chips, saving the remaining quarter to sprinkle on the top.

10. Pour into the pan and spread out evenly with a rubber spatula.

11. Bake for 25 minutes or until a fork stuck into the center comes out clean.

Chef's Note: You can choose to omit the cinnamon and swap the chocolate chili bar for a mint dark chocolate bar instead for a fresh twist.

PISTACHIO MINT TART

6–8

Truly a green dream! Loaded with soothing fresh mint, the aroma alone can be enough to lift you higher. Healthy fats from the pistachios and cashews provide a nutritious crunch. Avocado, coconut milk, and sweet honey blend up for a smooth, creamy filling that will make your skin glow.

Ingredients

CRUST

- 6 to 8 dates, pitted
- Filtered water
- 2½ cups raw pistachios
- ½ cup cacao nibs
- ¼ cup flaxseeds
- Pinch Celtic sea salt
- 1 teaspoon coconut oil

FILLING

- 3 medium avocados
- 1 (15-ounce) can coconut milk, chilled
- 2 cups shredded fresh coconut
- Juice of 1 lemon
- 1 whole vanilla bean, or 2 teaspoons vanilla extract
- ½ cup raw honey
- 3 cups packed fresh mint leaves, plus more for garnish

GARNISH

- 1 cup raw pistachios, chopped

Preparation

1. In a small bowl, soak the dates in filtered water for at least 30 minutes.

2. In a food processor, pulse the raw pistachios until mealy in texture. Add the cacao nibs, flaxseeds, and sea salt and process for about 15 seconds. With the motor running, add the soaked dates, one at a time, until the mixture forms a ball on one side of the bowl.

3. Using a paper towel and the coconut oil, lightly grease a 9" springform pan. Press the crust mixture into the base to form an even layer in the bottom of the pan.

4. Place in the freezer to set for 10 to 12 minutes while you assemble the filling.

5. To a Vitamix, add the avocados (pitted and peeled), hardened coconut milk (discarding the liquids), raw honey, lemon juice, vanilla bean or extract, and coconut. Add the mint leaves on top. Blend on low first and then increase the speed to thoroughly puree the mixture, using the plunger to evenly distribute the filling.

6. Remove the crust from the freezer and pour in the filling. Using a spatula, distribute the filling evenly and smooth the surface.

7. Return to the freezer for at least 2 hours. Thaw the pie for 30 minutes before serving. Carefully remove the outer ring of the springform pan and press chopped pistachios around the sides. Garnish with fresh mint and pistachios.

Chef's Note: You shouldn't be able to taste the avocado. Add another squeeze of lemon juice to neutralize any avocado taste.

RICH'S BIRTHDAY APPLE PIE

6-8

Rich enjoys this creation on his birthday as he is a lover of the "pie" and this one is his favorite. It's a fresh crisp taste that will feed your body and satisfy your sweet craving. The spiral of apples makes an impressive presentation. The secret is it's as easy as pie to make. The kids will want to help create this beautiful flower of thinly sliced sweet apples that will surely delight.

Ingredients

FILLING

- 6 apples (red, pink, or green local variety), cored and sliced in very thin sections

- 1 cup organic sugar

- ¼ cup arrowroot powder

- 1 teaspoon pumpkin pie spice or cinnamon

- Juice of 1 lemon

CRUST

- 2 cups raw walnuts

- Pinch Celtic sea salt

- ¼ cup ground flaxseeds

- 10 dates, soaked in filtered water for 30 minutes and pitted

- 1 teaspoon coconut oil

recipe continues >>

Preparation

1. Preheat the oven to 325°F.

2. Combine the apples with the sugar, arrowroot, spices, and lemon juice. Toss and set aside.

3. In a food processor, pulse the walnuts until mealy. Next, add the sea salt and pulse a few times. Add the flaxseeds and pulse again. With the motor running, drop one pitted date at a time into the processor. The mixture will ball up on one side of the bowl and form a dough.

4. Grease a 13" tart pan with the coconut oil. Press the crust mixture into the bottom of the pan.

5. Arrange the apples in a circular fashion starting at the edge. As you finish one round, begin again and add another layer and another until you finish creating a spiral flower pattern.

6. Bake for 40 minutes, or until the apples are soft and golden brown.

7. Remove from the oven and allow to cool.

8. Slice, serve, and enjoy with Coconut Ginger Ice Cream (page 266) or Cashew Vanilla Cream (page 81).

6–8

BLUEBERRY COSMIC CASHEW CHEESECAKE

Heavenly! This transcendental dessert will transport you out of this universe. Bursting with blueberries, lemon juice, silky tofu, and sweet raw honey, it's a magical mix of flavors. The nut-date crust is a delicious base for the creamy cashew cheesecake on top. The powerhouse blueberries pack a healthy dose of fiber; vitamins A, C, and E; plus selenium; zinc; and phosphorus, which are very good for glowing skin. Tofu and nuts give you added protein and healthy fats. This is a healthy way to satisfy any sweet tooth. Go ahead and create this cheesecake for someone you love.

Ingredients

CRUST

- 1 teaspoon coconut oil
- 1½ cups raw cashews
- Filtered water
- 6 to 8 dates
- Pinch Celtic sea salt

FILLING

- 1½ cups raw cashews
- Filtered water
- Juice of 2 lemons
- 1 tablespoon coconut oil
- 1 tablespoon soy or sunflower lecithin
- ⅔ cup blue agave
- 1 (12-ounce) package silken tofu
- 1 (10-ounce) package frozen blueberries, thawed, excess liquid drained, or 1 pint fresh blueberries

GARNISH

- Mint leaves

Preparation

1. Lightly grease a 9" springform pan with coconut oil.

2. In a medium bowl, soak the cashews (for the filling) in filtered water for at least an hour. Drain and set aside.

3. In a separate bowl, soak the dates (for the crust) in filtered water for at least a half hour. Remove the pits from the dates; set aside.

4. In a food processor, pulse the dry cashews and salt (for the crust) until mealy in texture. With the motor running, add the pitted soaked dates until the dates are mixed in.

5. Press the crust into the bottom of the prepared springform pan or glass pie dish. Place inside the freezer for 10 to 12 minutes or until firm.

6. Add the soaked cashews, lemon juice, coconut oil, soy or sunflower lecithin, blue agave, and silken tofu to a Vitamix or high-powered blender and let run on high for a few minutes, until the mixture has become a smooth blend.

7. Pour the blend into the crust and even out the top with a rubber spatula. Place back inside the freezer for a minimum of 2 hours, or until firm.

8. Remove from the freezer, gently release the springform buckle, and lift it off the cheesecake. Thaw for 30 minutes before serving. Arrange the blueberries on top. Garnish with mint leaves and serve.

Chef's Note: If you want a taller cheesecake, top with a layer of Coconut Honey Cream (page 80).

SUPERFOOD ENERGY BALLS

Sweet, chocolaty, and nutty rolled into one. These energy bites are really quick and easy to make and take on the go. Packed with nutrients such as zinc, calcium, magnesium, iron, omega-3 fats, and antioxidant-rich cacao, these bites are a family favorite. Try this version or experiment on your own using organic ingredients that you have on hand. Say yes to your sweet tooth and feed your beautiful body temple.

Ingredients

- 8 dates
- ½ cup raw walnuts
- 1 sprinkle Celtic sea salt
- ¼ cup cacao nibs
- 2 tablespoons raw cacao powder
- 4 tablespoons hemp seeds
- 1 teaspoon vanilla extract

Preparation

1. Begin by soaking the dates for 30 minutes. Pit and set aside.

2. In a food processor, pulse the walnuts until they are mealy in texture.

3. Add the sea salt, cacao nibs, cacao powder, and 2 tablespoons of the hemp seeds. Pulse until well incorporated.

4. With the food processor running, add the vanilla and the pitted dates one at a time until the mixture begins to form a dough.

5. Make small balls by rolling 2 tablespoons of the dough between your hands. If your hands get sticky, use a small amount of coconut oil on your palms.

6. Place the remaining 2 tablespoons hemp seeds on a plate and roll the Energy Balls in the hemp seeds to form an outer layer.

Chef's Note: Try adding a dash of cayenne pepper for a lively kick!

THE CREATIVE VOICE OF FOOD

What is cooking if not an art form? From the mandala of fresh whole foods and spices carefully selected for each dish to the mindful manner in which it is prepared, presented, and enjoyed, every meal is a unique manifestation of your authentic voice.

The recipes in this book offer you a firm foundation of knowledge so you can jump off into nature's kaleidoscope of flavors to heal, energize, and inspire. Connecting to your deeper intuition through creativity is really all about the process and not necessarily about knowing your end point. Or in this case, how the food will taste. Let go and enjoy the journey.

Allow yourself to take some risks in the kitchen. Try dishes that speak to you. Modify our recipes to include that colorful veggie that caught your eye at the market this morning. Infuse a dish with a specific mood by improvising with your favorite fresh herbs. Be free and unencumbered in your cooking style. Break the rules like a rock star! My point is that *there is no right or wrong*—only infinite possibilities to embrace and explore. If you attempt something that doesn't quite work, it's still a valuable experience—congratulations for trying! Don't sweat the details. Choose to fail and learn something new. More important is the energy you bring to the process. Allow your love and good intentions to permeate your kitchen creations. You just might be amazed at how impactful your emotional state can be on the finished product. The more lovingly you prepare food for others, the more the food fairies will smile down upon you and the more wonderful your food will taste.

If you find yourself doubting your natural ability or wondering if you will ever be able to prepare food as well as me, it's time to reconsider. Grandmas, grandpas, moms, and dads have been cooking for their families since the beginning of time. How many of us can recall a dish one of our elders prepared, the mere aroma of which can vividly transport us back to our childhood? Passed down from generation to generation, recipes that survive the ages forge beautiful family traditions, transforming lives in the process. That's the power of great food. And yet few of those responsible for creating the legendary family recipes we so relish and share had any formal kitchen training whatsoever. The secret ingredient for a great family recipe that stands the test of time isn't a secret ingredient. And it's not skill, technique, or training either. *It's love.*

Of course, you won't ever be able to prepare food exactly the way I do. This is not because I am a better chef, but because it's a scientific impossibility. Each time a recipe meets with unique energy, the food is completely different. Even if you purchase the same ingredients, the peach you use is an entirely different peach from the one I used. As it is with the ingredients, so it is with the chef. The unique energy that you bring to a recipe is inextricably linked to its outcome. At the risk of sounding a bit "out there," the thoughts you harbor while cooking directly impact the taste and quality of the result. I truly believe that the main reason my kitchen creations stand out is because I embrace this notion wholeheartedly, exercising great care to exude love, compassion, and positivity throughout the process. Sometimes I even chant mantras for health and well-being while I cook!

There is an ancient story from yogic lore about a devotee who prepared the same food for his master day after day, month after month, and year after year. Finally the servant couldn't stand it any longer. Continuously serving the same food was driving him crazy. He mustered the courage to question his master. "How can you stand eating the same food day after day, year after year? Aren't you tired of eating the same thing?" To this the master replied, "You have misunderstood. My food is never the same. It is unique and different each and every moment."

Unlike a painting or a sculpture, food is an impermanent, fleeting art form. A momentary artistic offering, the enjoyment of which necessitates its destruction. Taking the expression into your body, it quite literally becomes you, permanently transforming both artifact and receiver in the process. *Profound, right?* Let's reflect on this for a moment. The preparation and sharing of food is very much like performance art. It will not stay hanging on a wall or recorded for all time. It will be shared by however many dinner guests you have at your table. One time, then it's done. Taken in this context, it's easier to understand why I approach cooking as a truly spiritual offering, completely of the moment.

Taking the extra time to extend your artistic expression from the food and onto your table is a glorious homage to the meals you prepare. Make sure you have plenty of fresh green herbs, edible fruits, and flowers to garnish your dishes and adorn your table in natural beauty. Don't your creations deserve it? Invest energy to create perfect table settings to highlight the meal. I like to source unique items for this purpose. Family hand-me-downs and vintage-store treasures merge beautifully with your favorite modern plates. Mixing and blending aesthetics will give your table a tailored, authentic flair you simply can't achieve with a uniform, store-bought display. I also love the feel of handmade ceramics, which connect my soul with the earth. During some of my hardest moments in life, the simple feel of a warm clay teacup in

my hands has offered me deep comfort. Candles add a layer of ambience that can render the simplest family meal special and intimate. We always use clean-burning soy candles. They cast a soft light on our table and set the tone for a nourishing experience.

Finally, take a moment to create that perfect playlist. Adding a gentle backdrop sets the proper mood for your dining experience. And mood is everything. The more creative you are in your mealtime arrangements and the more you encourage and involve the entire family in the process, the more engaged and enthusiastic your children will be to contribute to precious family time together.

In our house, Tyler and Trapper usually provide the playlist or perform live music before or after dinner. Mathis has become great with making one-of-a-kind centerpieces from our garden. And our youngest one, Jaya, offers the meal blessing, followed by having us each say what we are grateful for.

Think you're not an artist? Of course you are! Everyone has something special to offer. Go for it! Creative expression is what makes a meal, in a word, *beautiful*. Go ahead and find your creative voice in food and feel the power it has to transform your dining experience.

Peace and blessings, from our table to yours.

LIFE + STYLE

LIFESTYLE PATHS
LIVING THE PLANTPOWER WAY

Living the Plantpower Way is a lifestyle approach that will cultivate long-term, truly self-sustainable living. Because we are all uniquely created, our interests and goals in adopting this lifestyle will vary from person to person. In this section we've identified three paths (or portals of entry) to support you in experiencing wholeness of mind, body, and spirit. We are all at different places in our journey along the path to true **vibrant** living. So this is an ever-changing and evolving process—both revolutionary and evolutionary!

Follow the path you feel best fits where you are right now in your life. Your choice of portal (or life path) is only a starting point, as inevitably all paths are interconnected and lead into each other at some point in the journey. For example, if you are living for **Vitality**, you will likely experience **Performance** and **Transformation**. If you are living for **Performance**, you will certainly experience **Vitality** and **Transformation**. If you are living for **Transformation**, you will also experience enhanced **Performance** and increasing **Vitality**. So go ahead! Pick one, and come on in! Welcome to discovering your best authentic self!

What if more than one path resonates with me? If a recipe isn't in my lifestyle path, does this mean I can never eat it? Most of us connect to more than one life path. Like we said, all paths will eventually lead into one another. So don't worry, you'll get a piece of all three. We offer these life plans simply to get you started. And it's likely that one of these paths speaks to your core more than the other two. Use this section as a guide. If you see a recipe from another path that calls to you, go ahead and eat it every now and then. Our focus is merely to emphasize the foods you will want to be eating regularly. For instance, if you are on the Phoenix Path, you will not want to be eating mashed potatoes and tons of nut- and avocado-based desserts. You will want to skip the oil as much as possible. But if you are on the Herbivore Path, you will need these extra calories to keep you fueled for training and racing. If you are on the Lotus Path, you won't want to be eating veggie burgers with a bread bun, peanut butter cookies, and mashed potatoes on a daily basis. Find your focus: is your food for vitality, performance, or transformation?

Vitality

Lotus Path · Food=Energy

This lifestyle path is characterized by balance and moderation, maintaining neutrality between the Yin and Yang. On this path, you are simply eating to live. Foods you eat should be pure energy. Focus is given to meals that are easily digested so you conserve and maximize the vital life force of your body and soul. This approach is inherently spiritually based and intended to activate expanded awareness in your life.

Performance

Herbivore Path · Food=Fuel

This lifestyle path is conceived to maximize physical performance. On this path, you are eating to fuel your body. Focus is on optimum performance and recovery. Athletes, teenagers, and the very active fit this approach. This protocol emphasizes high-calorie, nutrient-dense foods that fuel your workouts, prepare you for tomorrow's training session, and help you tap into power you never knew you had.

Transformation

Phoenix Path · Food=Alchemy

This lifestyle path is formulated to promote complete transformation. On this path, you will completely reboot your microbial gut ecology and metamorphose into your best authentic self. Chewing your food, juicing, and superfoods are the elements of your alchemy. This approach is calling forth your inner phoenix; soon you'll be rising from the ashes in your full expression.

VITALITY
THE LOTUS PATH

Congratulations on choosing the mindful approach toward living and embodying the Plantpower Way.

The key to this lifestyle approach is embracing the idea that food is energy. The quality of energy held by the foods we eat has a profound effect on not only the body but the mind and spirit as well. Moreover, the way in which food is prepared —including the chef's energy, emotional state, and intentions—also significantly impact the quality of the end product.

This path is about raising the vibration of our preparation and plate. It's about focusing on high-quality, nutrient-dense but easily assimilated foods that minimize digestive stress and maximize vitality.

Increasing mindfulness regarding the foods we choose and the rituals surrounding their preparation can have a profoundly positive impact on our energy, stress levels, sleep, and overall health.

Begin your day with quiet meditation accompanied by one of our calming hot morning teas or lattes. For breakfast, pass on the pancakes and opt for high-vibe juices and blends. The largest nourishment should come during the lunch hour; opt for lightly cooked foods to ease digestion. Throughout the day, drink at least eight glasses of water to keep you hydrated and flowing. For a mid-afternoon treat, try superfood sweets followed by a light dinner in the early hours of the evening (we prefer before 6:30 p.m.). Thirty minutes before climbing into bed, treat yourself to a warm calming tea as a final loving gift to the self before drifting off into a deep and peaceful sleep.

A Day in the Life

What follows is a typical day on the Lotus Path. Use this loosely as a guide, and feel free to customize it to suit your individual needs.

4:30–6:00 Arise. Drink a large glass of water with a squeeze of lemon. Wash your hands and face and brush your teeth. Practice JAI Release meditation (see Resources).

7:00 Enjoy a warm tea or latte to start your day.

8:30 Juice: Turmeric Orange Ginger

10:30 Monk Blend

12:30 Lunch: One Bowl

2:30 Energy Balls

6:30 Dinner: Superfood Pad Thai

8:30 Warm cup of nut milk with honey and cardamom

9:00 Practice JAI Release meditation

9:30 Sleep

PERFORMANCE
THE HERBIVORE PATH

Congratulations on choosing the warrior path of cultivating power, strength, and resilience in your journey into the Plantpower Way.

This approach emphasizes foods that empower the active lifestyle, minimize fatigue, and expedite recovery from exercise-induced stress so you can push your body day in and day out. Prioritizing nutrient-dense recipes high in anti-inflammatory antioxidants, protein, and healthy complex carbohydrates, this protocol will allow you to access reserves of previously undiscovered, boundless energy. In fact, the Herbivore Path is Rich's nutritional secret weapon, fueling him through countless hours of grueling training and ultra-endurance racing success.

Begin your day with a meditation visualizing success. Don't limit yourself—you are capable of far more than you ever imagined. Go crazy with greens and superfoods. Choose alkalizing fare low on the food chain to keep energy high, stave off illness, and combat inflammation. Indulge in Ultra Queen K Performance and EPIC5 Recovery Blends to repair the body temple and propel you like a powerful rhino to your next personal best.

A Day in the Life
What follows is a typical day on the Herbivore Path. Use this loosely as a guide, and feel free to customize it to suit your individual needs.

7:00 Arise and drink a glass of water with 1 tablespoon apple cider vinegar. Then visualize your workout or winning race and set your intentions of excellence for the day. Journal after.

7:30 Ultra Queen K Performance Blend

8:30 Morning training session

11:00 Epic 5 Recovery Blend

12:00 Lunch: Veggie Burgers with sweet potato fries

2:30 Superfood sweet-energy bars

4:30 Evening training session

7:00 Dinner: Aromatic Country-Style Tempeh Loaf, Hula Kale Salad, Mashed Potatoes

8:30 Meditation—visualize your body being completely healed, repaired, and upgraded.

9:30 Mint tea

10:00 Sleep

Recipes

Mains + Sides

Lattes + Teas

Treats + Sweets

TRANSFORMATION
THE PHOENIX PATH

Congratulations on choosing to be transformed on your journey into the Plantpower Way!

Ready to wipe the slate clean and begin anew? Then this path is for you. Let's begin the process of complete transformation by detoxifying the body and completely repopulating the microbial ecology living in your gut with a healthy life force that will shift your cravings and assist in breaking the vicious cycle of unhealthy eating habits—essential for optimum health. The key to this lifestyle approach is to cut out all oils, unhealthy fats, processed foods, gluten, and refined sugars. We replace these foods with the healing energy of vibrant living plants, plants, and more plants. The focus is on two green drinks a day—that's one juice and one blend—along with oil-free, nut-

free, warming meals and a reward of superfood sweets. In place of bread, upgrade to blanched collard greens or lettuce leaves to wrap any sandwich or veggie burger. Do your very best to go oil free wherever possible (we know it's hard), and make sure to go easy on the nuts. The largest meal is at noon and all meals should be eaten before 6:30 p.m. Make sure you drink at least eight glasses of lemon water a day to keep you hydrated, flowing, and alkalized. Beginning and ending your day with meditation will help harmonize any mental and emotional imbalances and better connect you with your inner alchemy as your body paves a new course to thrive.

A Day in the Life

What follows is a typical day on the Phoenix Path. Use this loosely as a guide, and feel free to customize it to suit your individual needs.

4:30–6:30 Arise, drink a glass of water with 1 tablespoon apple cider vinegar, wash your face and hands, and brush your teeth. Practice JAI Release meditation program (see Resources).

7:00 Mint Honey Hemp Latte

8:30 Green Juice

10:00 Morning Porridge

12:00 Cleansing Beet Soup, mixed grain pilaf

3:00 Deep Blue Sea Blend

6:00 Raw Kale Salad, Vegan Lasagna

8:30 Warm Rose Tea

9:00 Practice JAI Release meditation program

9:30 In bed

10:00 Sleep

RECIPE INDEX

JULIE PIATT

A true renaissance artist, Julie Piatt is the creative force behind her Ultraman husband, Rich Roll, and his amazing transformation. Vegan chef, healer, musician, yogi, and mother, Julie has traveled many paths and studied many traditions to find the *divine through line* in all her endeavors. Through embracing a Plantpower lifestyle, Julie healed herself of what doctors thought was an incurable ailment. This experience proved to her the miraculous ability of the body to restore itself to health when properly supported. *The Plantpower Way* is inspired by Julie's desire to share her deep connection to food as fuel for the body temple. Offering wise counsel on diet, family, relationships, and the power of unconditional love and unwavering faith, Julie promotes a whole lifestyle approach to healthy, creative, and authentic living. In addition, under her spiritual name SriMati, Julie has released two albums, *Mother of Mine* and *Jai Home*, both of which she recorded with her teenage sons, Tyler and Trapper.

srimati.com

facebook.com/srimatimusic

twitter.com/srimati

instagram.com/srimati

RICH ROLL

After finding himself sedentary and overweight in middle age, Rich overhauled his life at age forty, adopted a Plantpowered lifestyle, and reinvented himself as an ultra-distance endurance athlete. He went on to clock top finishes at the Ultraman World Championships and cemented his place in the pantheon of endurance greats when he was the first of two people to complete EPIC5—five ironman-distance triathlons on five Hawaiian Islands in under a week. His inspirational memoir *Finding Ultra: Rejecting Middle Age, Becoming One of the World's Fittest Men, and Discovering Myself* was an Amazon number one best seller and has inspired thousands across the world to embrace a Plantpowered approach to diet, fitness, and life. Rich has been profiled on CNN and in countless magazines, was named one of the "25 Fittest Men in the World" by *Men's Fitness,* and is the host of *The Rich Roll Podcast,* one of the world's most popular podcasts with many millions of downloads. A graduate of Stanford University and Cornell Law School, Rich is an inspiration to people worldwide as a transformative example of healthy living.

richroll.com

facebook.com/richrollfans

twitter.com/richroll

The Rich Roll Podcast on iTunes

instagram.com/richroll

GRATITUDE

A great recipe is so much more than its individual ingredients. As it is with food, so it is with the creation of this book.

The Plantpower Way marks a huge milestone in our family journey—a journey that has been indelibly shaped by so many beautiful souls, all committed to the ideal that together we can foster a better way of life for ourselves, our children, and the planet at large. This book is a physical manifestation of that ideal.

To Greg, Yvonne, Julian, and Kyra Anzalone, thank you for believing in us, for stepping into our lives and blessing us with your pure hearts and expanded vision of a better world. Your mentorship, influence, guidance, friendship, and unwavering support continue to elevate us all to higher ground. Words cannot express the extent of our heartfelt gratitude for the positive impact you continue to have on our family.

To Sanjay Gupta, thank you for taking such a keen interest in our mission; thank you for so freely sharing our story with the world; thank you for your example and mentorship; thank you for your commitment to a better, healthier world; and of course, thank you for your touching and thoughtful contribution to this book.

Responsibility for the beautiful layout, look, and feel of *The Plantpower Way* rests with our young and talented graphic designer, Shawn Patterson. Thank you for all the patience, care, time, and attention to quality that you invested in us and this project. We are beyond lucky to have you on our team.

Remarkably, almost every recipe image in this book was captured in a mere two-day period. Despite our incredibly ambitious production schedule, we are thrilled with the extraordinary food photography produced by our well-oiled team. Thank you, Ginny Guzman, for your uniquely brilliant eye. Thank you, Stephanie Farrell, for your food-styling touch. Thank you, Jules Tolentino, Diego Pacheco, Trapper, and Tyler, for keeping the kitchen humming and food prep running smoothly. And thank you to our beloved and recently passed golden retriever, Bodhi, for your repeated photo-bombing and for keeping our floor scrap-free. You will be missed, dear prince.

Lifestyle photography thanks go to the extraordinary Maclay Heriot, who took a break from shooting rock stars to capture our family. Maclay, your candid, documentary-style aesthetic infuses these pages with a youthful vitality and originality that cannot be replicated. Mad respect also goes out to our talented photographer friends John Segesta and Tom Medvedich for their uber-action shots of Rich. Thank you also to Amanda Sloane for the wonderful image of Sanjay that adorns our foreword. And for keeping Julie beautiful, thank you, Dedra Dakota and Jenny Halprin.

Of course, a huge debt of gratitude extends to the team at Avery. Thank you, Lucia Watson, for elevating every aspect of our work, for believing in our potential, for your steady stewardship, and for being true to your word. Thank you,

Gigi Campo, for staying on top of every detail. Lindsay Gordon, Anne Kosmoski, and Farin Schlussel, thank you for refusing to stop until everyone on earth knows about the book. And to everyone else working behind the Avery curtain, thank you for helping craft our dream into a reality.

Thank you, Isabel Snyder (and your donkeys), for welcoming our shoot into your beautiful home. And thank you, Morgan Hopp, for letting us shoot at the beautiful and truly one-of-a-kind One Gun Ranch in Malibu, high above the Pacific.

Thank you, Stephen and Michael Lubin and Matthew Groves, for capturing the production on film and creating our amazing trailer video. Thank you, Lynda Layng, for your invaluable editorial assistance with the recipes. Gratitude to Ron Capri and Lili Foster for helping test the recipes. And thank you, copyeditor Lisa Marquart, for catching every error our eyes didn't.

Thanks, Saul David Raye, for your friendship and support, for fanning Julie's culinary spark, and for giving her the confidence to share her food creations beyond the family table.

Also, our gratitude goes out to the venerable Sri Swami Vidyadhishananda for your Ayurvedic nutritional information and Pranic lifestyle guidance. And of course, thank you, June Louks, for your friendship, support, and raw-food nutritional inspiration.

The Plantpower Way was originally intended to be self-published. That was until our friend Mishka Shubaly insisted we meet his agent. Byrd Leavell came into our lives and everything changed. Thank you, Mishka, for your friendship, for believing in us, and for constantly bullying Rich to break new ground as a writer. To Byrd, thank you for your steady counsel, for your confidence in our mission, and for your vision for this book and beyond.

Thank you, Raoul Goff, for your expert feedback and selfless, steadfast mentorship of this project at every stage of development from concept to cover. We could never repay you for the invaluable input you have graciously imparted.

And finally, we wish to thank the countless unnamed all over the world who read *Finding Ultra*, listened to the podcast, found a spark of hope in our story, or took the time to share with us your private struggles and triumphs. You simply cannot imagine how much you have touched our lives. And to all those out there who feel stuck, lost, in a rut, or just unable to transcend habits or behaviors that no longer serve you, understand that we are with you. You are all an integral and vital part of this movement. Keep rising. We are with you in each breath and in every moment. This book is for you.

Peace, plants, and namaste!

Rich, Julie, Tyler, Trapper, Mathis, and Jaya

RESOURCES*
Our Products & Services

The Rich Roll Podcast
Website, www.richroll.com/category/podcast
iTunes, https://itunes.apple.com/us/podcast/the-rich
-roll-podcast/id582272991?mt=2
Soundcloud, www.soundcloud.com/richroll
Stitcher Radio, www.stitcher.com/podcast/30437

Online Educational Video Courses
*The Ultimate Guide to Plant-Based Nutrition with Rich
Roll and Julie Piatt*
www.mindbodygreen.com/course/the-ultimate
-guide-to-plant-based-nutrition

The Art of Living with Purpose with Rich Roll
www.mindbodygreen.com/course/the-art-of-living
-with-purpose

Digital Products
Jai Seed eCookbook, by Rich Roll and Julie Piatt
www.richroll.com/products/jai-seed-ecookbook

Jai Release Guided Meditation Program, by Julie Piatt
www.richroll.com/products/jai-release-meditation-
program

Nutritional Products
Repair—Plantpower Protein Supplement
www.richroll.com/products/repair-plantpower
-protein-supplement

B_{12} Spray
www.richroll.com/products/rich-rolls-b12
-supplement

ION Electrolyte Supplement
www.richroll.com/products/ion-electrolyte
-supplement

Apparel
www.richroll.com/apparel

Restaurant & Vegan, Gluten-Free Baked Goods and Desserts
Joi Café, www.joicafe.com
Karma Baker, www.karmabaker.com

Julie's Music
Website: www.srimati.com
Mother of Mine, www.cdbaby.com/cd/srimati or on iTunes
Jai Home, www.cdbaby.com/cd/jaihome or on iTunes

* With the exception of our own products and services, an associate producer association with *Cowspiracy,* and minority interests in Karma Baker and Joi Café, we have no financial relationship whatsoever with any of the authors, companies, products, services, films, or websites listed in Resources.

Plant-Based Nutrition Primers & Cookbooks

The China Study: The Most Comprehensive Study of Nutrition Ever Conducted and the Startling Implications for Diet, Weight Loss and Long-Term Health, T. Colin Campbell and Thomas M. Campbell II (BenBella Books, 2006)

Engine 2 Diet: The Texas Firefighter's 28-Day Save-Your-Life Plan That Lowers Cholesterol and Burns Away the Pounds, Rip Esselstyn (Grand Central, 2009)

Meat Is for Pussies: A How-To Guide for Dudes Who Want to Get Fit, Kick Ass, and Take Names, John Joseph (HarperWave, 2014)

My Beef with Meat: The Healthiest Argument for Eating a Plant-Strong Diet, Rip Esselstyn (Grand Central, 2013)

Neal Barnard's Program for Reversing Diabetes: The Scientifically Proven System for Reversing Diabetes Without Drugs, Dr. Neal D. Barnard (Rodale Books, 2008)

Thrive Energy Cookbook: 150 Plant-Based Whole Food Recipes, Brendan Brazier (Da Capo Press, 2014)

Thrive: The Vegan Nutrition Guide to Optimal Performance in Sports and Life, Brendan Brazier (Da Capo, 2008)

The Whole Heart Solution: Halt Heart Disease Now with the Best Alternative and Traditional Medicine, Joel Kahn MD (Readers Digest, 2014)

PLANTPOWER-FRIENDLY WEBSITE RESOURCES

Rich Roll, www.richroll.com

NutritionFacts, www.nutritionfacts.org

Physicians Committee for Responsible Medicine, www.pcrm.org

Mind Body Green, www.mindbodygreen.com

NoMeatAthlete, www.nomeatathlete.com

Food Politics, www.foodpolitics.com

Civil Eats, www.civileats.com

Fully Raw, www.fullyraw.com

Oh She Glows, www.ohsheglows.com

Post Punk Kitchen, www.theppk.com

Sprouted Kitchen, www.sproutedkitchen.com

Meatless Monday, www.meatlessmonday.com

Engine 2 Diet, www.engine2diet.com

T. Colin Campbell Center for Nutrition Studies, www.nutritionstudies.org

Dr. Dean Ornish, www.ornishspectrum.com

Dr. Caldwell Esselstyn, www.heartattackproof.com

Lifeforce + Lifestyle Workbook: Practical Teachings of Atharvaveda and Ayurveda by Sri Swami Vidyadhishananda, www.swamahiman.org

Dr. John McDougall, www.drmcdougall.com

Dr. Joel Fuhrman, www.drfuhrman.com

RECOMMENDED FILMS

Cowspiracy, www.cowspiracy.com

Forks Over Knives, www.forksoverknives.com

Fed Up, www.fedupmovie.com

Genetic Roulette, www.geneticroulettemovie.com

Food, Inc., www.foodincmovie.com

Foodmatters, www.foodmatters.tv

King Corn, www.kingkorn.net

Super Size Me, www.hulu.com/watch/63283

Vegucated, www.getvegucated.com

The Future of Food, www.thefutureoffood.com

Fat, Sick and Nearly Dead, www.fatsickandnearlydead.com

Fat, Sick & Nearly Dead 2, www.fatsickandnearlydead.com

An imprint of Penguin Random House, LLC
375 Hudson Street
New York, New York 10014

Most Avery books are available at special quantity discounts for bulk purchase for sales promotions, premiums, fund-raising, and educational needs. Special books or book excerpts also can be created to fit specific needs. For details, write SpecialMarkets@penguinrandomhouse.com.

ISBN: 978-1-58333-5-871

Printed in the United States of America
3   5   7   9   10   8   6   4   2

Neither the publisher nor the author is engaged in rendering professional advice or services to the individual reader. The ideas, procedures, and suggestions contained in this book are not intended as a substitute for consulting with your physician. All matters regarding your health require medical supervision. Neither the author nor the publisher shall be liable or responsible for any loss or damage allegedly arising from any information or suggestion in this book.

The recipes contained in this book have been created for the ingredients and techniques indicated. The publisher is not responsible for your specific health or allergy needs that may require supervision. Nor is the publisher responsible for any adverse reactions you may have to the recipes contained in the book, whether you follow them as written or modify them to suit your personal dietary needs or tastes.

While the author has made every effort to provide accurate telephone numbers, Internet addresses, and other contact information at the time of publication, neither the publisher nor the author assumes any responsibility for errors, or for changes that occur after publication. Further, the publisher does not have any control over and does not assume any responsibility for author or third-party websites or their content.